THE W/ALL

SEASON 1

Antoine "Don Twan" Robinson

Copyright © 2016 by Antoine "Don Twan"Robinson ISBN: 978-0-9966252-2-7 LCCN: 2016931686

Legit Styles Publishing 16501 Shady Grove Rd Suite# 7562 Gaithersburg, MD 20898 info@legitstylespublishing.com legitstylespublishing.com

Join Us on Social Media

The Legit Styles

The Legit Styles

Legit Styles Publishing

DEDICATIONS

To my nephew Anthony Christophe` Edward Lebrane, let this book be my first lesson to you. You can accomplish anything that you put your mind to.

To my Uncle Todd Robinson, in Colorado State Prison, keep your head up. I'll be home soon to help you in every way possible.

To Byron "CEO" Grey, stay focused and know that your energy and effort will never go unnoticed. I truly appreciate you. I love you like family and that's from the heart.

To my mother, Paula Robinson, I love you Boobie! You are My sunshine..My world..My universe.

CAST

Jim Dempster...............................Warden

Trevor Maddox...........................AW/Warden

Captain McDaniels......................Captain

Richard Frost.............................Lieutinant

Tina Frost..................................Nurse

James Carson............................Case Manager

Adam.......................................Rookie C.O.

Ted Gibbs................................Veteran C.O.

Hal Shriver..............................Veteran C.O.

Leon Taylor............................Veteran C.O.

Alexis Green...........................Rookie C.O.

Erin Jiminez...........................Rookie C.O.

Dino......................................Convict/Hustler

Maniak..................................OG Blood

Bone.....................................OG Crip

Donnie Ru.............................YG Piru

Big Jake...............................Whites Shotcaller

Asian Lee...Asian Shotcaller

Joe-Joe..D.C./Convict

Petey Moe..D.C./Convict

Gordo...Paisa Shotcaller

Biker Dan..Dopefiend

SUPPORTING CAST

Officer Rosalez	Chris	Champ
Snake	Jason	Fats
Skull	Tray	Ty
Critter	Jinx	Dingo
Lucky	Butta	Slim
Meech	Twan	Gator
Lil' B		

THEATER OF WAR

"Rosalez, good morning." The officer working the front desk in the administration building spoke as he did to everyone else. It was more out of habit than proper etiquette. Ignoring him, Rosalez cleared the metal detector all the correctional officers had to pass through before going onto the compound. Without a simple glance, he clutched his Jansport backpack, coasting past several other employees.

"Dammit, Hal! I'm not giving you back the hundred if you don't turn in your roster. Today's the final day for all fantasy teams."

"Yeah Hal. Just pick from the remaining players. Who knows, you just might luck up and win the whole pot."

Hal looked at the two men speaking. Ted was a fantasy football junky who ran a pool every year. Leon, the playa-playa ladies' man, only played because Ted pressured all of them to. Hell, he didn't know why he gave Ted the $100 in the first place.

"Alright, give me until lunch."

"That'ah boy. Hey Rozi, how 'bout you? Are you playing this year," Ted smiled and said.

Just like the fat ass working the desk, Rosalez paid Ted and his crew no mind. His only response came in the form of a stone face, etched with hard lines. With his eyes fixed before him, like a man on a mission, he came to the glass doors that led through the building, pushing his way forward.

It was 6:30 a.m. and like every work day the place was slowly coming alive. Officers that worked graveyard shift were clocking out while their reliefs came in sipping hot cups of cappuccino and coffee. Unlike the rest, Rosalez walked the hallways like he normally did. He was the quiet type so no one thought it suspicious when he walked by without speaking. The two secretaries he always saw conversing about their single parenting issues and the small groups of officers here and there, amped for another day of prison life-each of them knew his face well.

But not him as a person. Not one bit.

9

Once he passed through the administration building, Rosalez came to a metal door that was controlled by an old veteran named Captain Foley. Although he never made the rank in his thirty something years working in the prison system, this was what they called him.

"Well, good morning, youngster," the old captain said in his signature greeting.

Rosalez looked up at him and nodded. He was the only one in the whole prison he felt was sincere.

In the 365 days he had worked there, Mr. Foley was the only person he spoke to saying,"Good morning to you as well."

The old man nodded back and pressed the buzzer, unlocking the door.

A light chill blanketed the compound. Although the forecast was for temperatures around 90 degrees by high noon, the sun was barely coming up. Rosalez moved about the walkway as other officers trekked to and from the units they worked. It was still during breakfast time so some inmates were out as well, coming in and out of the chow hall.

Everything was routine as he looked up at the gun tower hovering in the center of the yard. The distinctive shadow of a figure silhouetted the mirrored glass.

"A-Yard is closed," was announced from the tower. This was proper protocol for when one officer was relieving another of the tower's post. They always cleared that yard.

This also told him the guy working up there had seen him coming. *What a blast this is gonna be,* he thought.

As inmates scurried to get through the gate and off of A-Yard, Rosalez entered the unauthorized area. The officer in the tower buzzed him into the gated area. Once in, he closed the gate then went to the door, where he was buzzed in as well. Inside was a circular staircase, which he took until he came to the epicenter of the tower.

The Control Room.

"Well hell," the officer announced. "You're about the most prompt relief I've had all quarter."

The man was in his early 50's, black, sported a popped belly, and was baldhead. A well-manicured salt and pepper goatee was cut upon his face. Setting his backpack down, Rosalez took his federal issued cap with the *Bureau of Prison* insignia upon it and tossed it on the desk by the controls. Beyond that, the view of the prison compound and grounds laid beneath them.

"Just let me grab my things and it's all yours," the officer told him as he moved about the booth's small space. "Have you worked this post before?"

With his eyes bouncing from corner to corner, Rosalez grew familiar with the area, and replied, "Actually, I have not."

The man paused and looked at him then shaking his head he said, "Figures. Well, to your right over there in that corner are your concussion grenades, ammo, and such." He pointed slightly to the right where a cage was mounted. "And there are the M-Sixteen's and riot pumps."

Rosalez moved to the cage and opened it.

"Yeah, trust and believe you'll need those. These boys here are the most dangerous sons'ah bitches in the whole country. When they get fixed and ready, a knife fight or riot will break out at any moment."

While the man spoke, his fingers traced the rubber grip of the shotgun. The M-16 looked powerful, a well manufactured killing machine.

"Yep," the officer continued. "So don't hesitate one bit." Picking up his half-empty lunch pail, he turned to Rosalez who was now holding the assault rifle. "Now that's a beauty, ain't it?"

With the magazine in place, Rosalez racked a round into its chamber. "Yes. Yes sir, it really is."

The man's eyes grew wide with horror as he saw the menacing look on the rifleman's face.

"Son you—"

No other words escaped his mouth as Rosalez squeezed the trigger, sending an echoing .223 bullet exploding from the barrel. Fire leaped as the projectile slammed into the officer's

11

face, sending his body lurching backward and onto the control boards. Blood and brain matter splattered the tinted windows of the tower. The single shot left a hole in the glass that sent splintering-spider webbed cracks from its center.

Lowering his weapon, Rosalez showed no expression or remorse. He simply grabbed the lifeless body by the ankle and pulled it towards a corner so he could get a good look at the view below.

Now he smiled. The first sign that he was happy to be at work.

Very happy indeed.

****

When the distress signal first initiated, Warden Dempster thought it to be an early morning drill being executed by either his Captain or Lieutenant. That's until he heard the announcement being repeated over his radio by control.

"Gunfire in the main tower! I repeat! Gunfire in Tower-A!"

"Honey, let me call you back. We have an issue up here," Warden Dempster stated.

His wife, Margret, had called to remind him of their 8 year old daughter's recital. If he missed it he would surely be sleeping in the doghouse with Stubbles. After 25 years in corrections, he promised his spouse he'd do right by raising the last of their three children. "Okay, hun," she said. "I'll see you at the theater."

"Five-thirty. I'll be there."

"On time."

"Yes, honey. Not a second later." Just as he hung up, his office door flew open. It was his assistant, Warden Trevor Maddox. The look on his face was of pure panic.

"Sir, Tower-A has been hijacked."

Warden Dempster's massive 285 pound frame flew to its full 6 foot 4 inch height. "What do you mean hijacked?" As he spoke, his porcelain complexion grew paler at the realization of his question.

"Our visual from Tower-C confirms an individual in Tower-A is pacing with a rifle in his hands."

"Who is it?"

"Hard to say. Jackson worked graveyard but was being relieved by Officer Jose Rosalez. So, it could be either one."

"Either one? Why not—"

"We believe one of them shot the other."

Wasting no more time, the Warden snatched his jacket from the back of his chair."Let's go!"

****

When the blast first sounded, Dino was just making it out of the chow hall. Even though he'd been down for ten years, he knew a gunshot when he heard one. The rapid *crack* cut into the conversation he was having with Donnie, a partner of his from Compton, California. Donnie was a hardcore Piru gang member in his early 30's and they were discussing money.

"What the fuck was that?"

Donnie flinched. The flash in his peripheral drew his attention to the tower."Look… up there."

Dino saw it too. A twisted feeling deep in his gut stood him up straight. "The tower?"

Donnie was still pointing. By this time, there was fifty inmates out on the yard. All of whom had stopped, growing completely silent.

Obvious cracks and a hole showed in the glass, confirming his worst fear. As a black man, nothing bothered Dino more than having an unstable officer suffering from post-traumatic stress up there working with live ammo. He could handle these con ass, jive gangbanging gangsters, but a killer with a badge was too much.

"You see that?" his friend asked. "A gun must've accidently went off up there. Look at that window. It's—"

13

When the sliding glass window of the tower opened, Donnie shut up and the wind stood still. A young looking Hispanic officer stood exposed from the waist up. In his hands was an M-16. For a moment, he seemed to take in the people on the compound. Then with the skill of a trained marksman, he leaned forward on the window's ledge for leverage, taking up aim with the weapon.

"Oh shit!"

Dino's words cut the silence, echoing loud off of the brick walls that encompassed them. The officer swung his weapon first left, then right, finally stopping on three white cats standing up against a unit's wall.

Plow!

The explicit visual of a guy's head erupting against the man next to him was enough to send every living soul darting for cover.

"This mutha'fucka is crazy!" Donnie said livid.

The gunman was only getting started as he sent another blast at his victim's fleeing friend.

Plow!

Donnie was now tugging on Dino's sweater. "Do you see—"

"Inside! Man, let's go," Dino yelled after seeing the second victim take a round to the torso.

Thankful to still be close to the doors by the chow hall, both men stepped inside the hallway. The sound of jingling keys grew to a concerted rhythm, drawing both of their attention towards the end of the hall. At least 15 officers rounded the corner with both Warden and AW in the pack.

"Inmates, get on the floor! Now!" an officer yelled out.

Both of them complied in a hurry.

"Look sir," the AW Maddox said. "He's taking up aim on inmates."

Dino kept his ears and eyes peeled.

Warden Dempster watched in horror as the gunman racked off another round at a lone man running for cover. The flash and *crack* of gunfire caused the head of the facility to jump himself. It was the way that the inmate's body contorted once the bullet struck him that gave the Warden a sense of adrenaline.

"Why in Jesus' name," he mumbled to himself. "Someone get me a bullhorn."

One of the three lieutenants on the scene stepped forward. "Here you are, sir."

Warden Dempster grabbed it without taking a single eye off the gunman. "What's his name again?"

"Jose Rosalez," Maddox said after seeing the Hispanic man.

The gunman fired off another round. This one ricocheted off the handball's court concrete wall. His target was a fleeing inmate, who God spared just in the nick of time.

"Okay listen," the Warden began. "Maddox, call the National Guard. Someone call an ambulance."

The AW and a lieutenant both ran off.

To another officer Warden Dempster barked, "Grab the door for me. I'ma see if I can catch his attention."

While all of this was playing out, Dino peeked from his place on the ground.

Doing as he was told, the officer opened the door. Right on cue, the Warden stepped into plain view, raising the bullhorn to his lips.

"Officer Rosalez! This is your Warden speaking. Whatever it is, I want you to think this through and—"

Plow!

All Dino saw was the explosion of the bullhorn as shards of plastic splintered towards his face. After blocking his head, he opened his eyes to see Warden Dempster's body lying in a dead heap. The other officers ducked for cover.

"Close the door! Close the got damn door!" one of them yelled.

With all the commotion that ensued, the shock of the massive man lying in an ever-growing pool of blood signaled the worst event Dino had seen in years. His worst fear had come to life, but instead with a deadly twist.

THE WALL

****

The year was 2001...
The sun hung high in the sky. The City of Kabul boasted a temperature of 112 degrees. Gunfire erupted from buildings, sending livestock of donkeys, goats, and sheep scurrying down dust filled roads. The Taliban militia lurked behind stonewalls and storefront windows discharging ammo at all U.S. Military forces who threatened to take down their regime for the September 11th attacks that occurred on the Twin Towers in New York City.

The place was a war zone.

Rosalez was a United States Marine with a Corporal rank deployed to the capitol city in Afghanistan. He was trained to be the best and today he'd be nothing less. When a missile was fired and struck the concrete structure him and his squad hid behind the effects sent shards of rubble, destroying the building's roof, killing all of his fellow officers. Now alone, he crouched with his M-16 looking for his assailants.

"Where are you, you son of a bitch," he growled, gritting his teeth.

The smoke blinded him from seeing clearly. He knew that the militia group was recruited as young children so anyone moving could be a potential threat.

Seeing movement behind a two-story building, Rosalez took aim. Someone dressed in traditional Muslim garb leaped from the shadows, wielding an AK-47 assault rifle.

"Aaalllahhh-u-akbarrrr!"

Rosalez was upon him, firing rapid shots and striking his enemy in the upper body. The terrorist immediately crumbled, sending puffs of dust to rise as his body fell.

One down and many to go.

"Help me, please! Help me!" a woman screamed.

Rosalez turned his attention towards the pleading voice and saw a helpless woman being led across the street as a shield by another terrorist.

16

"Let her go!" he yelled out.

The attacker refused. With a grenade in hand, he looked at Rosalez and stopped in the middle of the road.

"Allah-u-akbar!" he yelled, then he released the safety on the explosive device.

Rosalez ducked for cover.

Ka-Boom!

The deafening blast vibrated in his ears. The smell of sulfur and gunpowder filled his nostrils, along with the metallic scent of blood. When Rosalez turned and looked back, he saw four armed men emerge from the smoke. Their eyes were the only thing visible in their dark attire. Their automatic weapons shone steady as they took aim at his hiding place.

"Allah-u-akbarrr!" they screamed just before they opened fire.

Taking cover, Rosalez ducked as bullets ricocheted off the building.

His heart pounded as sweat poured down his face and soaked his uniform. The sound of women and children crying and yelling for help filled his ears. He was breathing heavily. *Get it together,* he thought himself. Then taking two deep breaths, he closed his eyes and gathered himself before gripping his rifle.

He turned, took aim to return fire but…..

All he saw was the inner complex of the prisons compound. He wiped the sweat from his eyes. The weapon in his hands shook as he assessed what was actually taking place before him. Dead bodies laid scattered out in different areas as inmates ran for cover. Backing from his perch on the gun tower window seal, Rosalez turned only to see the dead body of a fellow officer laid out in a corner filled with blood.

A theater of war.

His eyes scanned erratically as images were captured like random photographs in his mind. The control booth, the housing units, and correctional officers running onto the compound. All these and many more he saw. It was the sight of the American flag in the distance flying on a pole just outside the compounds exterior walls that caught his attention.

The home of the brave.

Finally, his heart stopped its rapid beating. A wave of calm came over him as his eyes stayed locked on the sight of the flag. Then, standing at attention, he saluted the symbol of freedom he fought for just before raising the barrel of the rifle beneath his chin.

"Hooo-Rah!" he roared before pulling the trigger, and finally ending the demons that haunted him.

WELCOME TO THE WALL

EPISODE 1
PRISON POLITICS

1

The year is 2020...

Located in Southeast California, and bordering the State of Nevada, is an area of desert called Death Valley. It stretches for 140 miles and is somewhere between 5 to 15 miles wide. Bounded on the west, by the Paramount Range, on the east by the Black Funeral and Grapevine Mountains of the Amargosa Range, this area of land is 95% uninhabited. The cause of this is due to one simple fact: it's the hottest place to live in America.

Boasting the highest recorded temperature in the nation of 134 degrees in 1931, Death Valley got its name from a group of settlers seeking gold in 1849. Ignorant to the desert's mass and heat, many travelers lost their lives, which prompted the name. Now, in more modern times, the desert sees summer temperatures yearly at 120 degrees.

One a hell of a place.

The Federal Bureau of Prisons or FBOP is a major prison industry that houses some of the most dangerous criminals the nation or international community has ever known; there are over 110 prisons. The more severe crimes find offenders housed in the high-level security facilities. These prisons are commonly located in some of the most remote areas available; places of non-descript and outside the reach of societies tax paying citizens.

The facilities at the highest level of custody are USP's or United States Penitentiary and ADMAX or Administration Maximum or ADX as it's commonly known. ADMAX facilities house convicts who require the tightest controls, many of which have major influence or high profile cases and sometimes both. USP's have highly secured perimeters, multiple housing units, higher staff to inmate ratios, and closer control of inmate's movement.

Throughout the 90's and early 2000's, California boasted two of the most violent USP's in the system named Atwater and USP-Victorville. When the lone ADMAX facility in Florence, Colorado was burned down as a result of the most violent riot the FBOP had ever witnessed, the big wigs in Washington, DC made a decision. They elected to close the Southern California USP-Victorville and resurrected a new USP/ADMAX in a place fitting for the violent offenders they'd house there.

That is in Death Valley, California.

Sitting on 14 ½ acres of dry desert land USP/ADMAX Death Valley is a fortress. With four perimeter gun towers that sit outside the prison, the facility keeps three truck patrollers constantly circling the outer area. Several electric bobbed wired fences sit multi-rowed, encircling the compound. Nothing stands in comparison to the 50 ft. wall that box off the joint. It is one of a kind, separating the criminals from the free world and stands as a symbol for the security it offers.

Thus, the prison is nicknamed *The Wall*.

Inside The Wall, the compound is no less spectacular with another gun tower sitting at its center— overseeing all movement, twelve housing units between buildings A, B, and C (four in each) making for inmate living quarters. The compound is separated by fences into three yards to decrease inmate interaction. Areas such as medical, dining hall, education, administrative offices, vocational training, chapel, and law library are all indoors and connected, helping to make up a square compound. The place had over 100 cameras inside and outside buildings and is designed with no blind spots. That way the officer working the gun tower can aim and hit anyone from any angle.

There are no indoor recreation departments and no indoor commissary building at the prison. If convicts wished to have recreation, they had to do so under the watchful eye of a gunman. If they spent their money, they did so knowing they can do so safely.

When Dino first arrived at USP-Death Valley, he was simply glad to be close to his family. Being from San Bernardino, CA put him only hours away from home. He had spent 7 years out of the ten he'd been down at USP-Pollock located in Central Louisiana. The first few months at Death Valley brought peace. Since it was scarcely populated, housing only 350 people. The spot was brand new and extremely quiet compared to the hostile prison he'd come from. *Bloody Pollock* was what it was nicknamed. That was a name it earned with high honors. It was one deadly place to do time.

Now things were changing. The word was The Wall was increasing its population and with that would come extreme changes. If the FBOP was going to bus or fly in more convicts then Dino knew some ground rules had to be established. So taking the initiative, he got with a couple of his partners from California and put a call out for all the shot callers and representatives of each group or car on the yard to meet up after breakfast. The call turned out to be successful and now he, along with 11 other reputables, stood outside to discuss the future of their new home.

A fence separated the group, splitting them into six on one side and five on the other side. The Bloods, Gangsta Disciples, Crips, White Boys, Latin Kings, Vice Lords, Mexican Mafia, Dirty South, Asians, East Coast, and California cars were all present. Dino was upset that the shot caller for the Paisas, named Gordo, couldn't be present due to a dentist appointment but Dino promised to fill him in.

"Good morning men," he said to them all.

"What up?"

"Good morning."

"Top of the mornin'."

Round and round came responses to the man they all knew.

"I asked all of y'all to come out so we could talk about these rumors we've all been hearing," he said. "As y'all have heard, they're supposed to be bussing in a bunch of new cats to the pound. Word is they're supposed to be emptying the holes from other USP's and sending them here."

"Yeah, they're saying this is going to be the new disciplinary facility for the Central and Western regions," Maniak said. He was the representative for the Bloods, a hardened criminal from the Belhaven Bounty Hunters in Watts.

Big Jake, The Butcher, nodded his head in agreement. "My brothers are sayin' buses should be coming in sometime this week or next week at the latest," he said.

"Has anyone heard how many?" Bone asked, representing the Crips and his gang the 4 Tray Gangsters.

"A couple hundred to start," Jake stated.

Dino knew that Big Jake stayed informed about certain things the rest of them weren't. The 6'7" 260 lbs. white boy was not only the shot caller of the whites; he had a name for being ruthless. Word was his life sentence came from a horrifying act he committed when he used a meat cleaver to chop up his brother and his wife, who he caught fucking in his bed. He chopped their bodies into parts, froze them in a deep freezer, and then fed them to his Bull Mastiffs. By the time, the authorities caught on, only the head of his wife, an arm, and two legs remained. From that point, the media gave him the moniker, *The Butcher.*

Not wanting to waste any time, Dino got straight to the point.

"My reason for calling all of you is simple. We've all been down and doing time and we all know how shit can get with these prison politics. This is a new spot and if what we're hearing is true, a lot of crazy mutha'fuckas are on the way. Some are my people, some are yours." He paused to make sure they all understood. "Now," he continued. "It's been peaceful so far. We all got our shit goin' between gamblin' and dope. You know, we doin' what we do and that's how it's going to be. Once our people get off that bus it's up to us to make sure they understand that there is a level of respect that we've built amongst each other."

Spike was a GD out of Chicago, who totally understood Dino's point. "Aye folks, I feel like this," he began. "Let 'cho people know that if they got a problem with any of mine, find anyone of my people to bring it to before they take matters into their own hands."

"Exactly," came Paco who was the shot caller for the Mexican Mafia. "That will keep a lot of things from goin' bad around here."

Gator was from Florida and represented for the Dirty South car. A veteran who had been down for over 30 years, he stood strong and sturdy for a man of 62 years old. "I'm hearin' dem boys outta DC are comin'. Ain't one of dem on this 'pound to speak for amongst us. We all know they can be a problem."

Dino had heard that some cats from Washington, DC were indeed coming. With a reputation for being a ruthless bunch, it drew some concern but not much. They were all ruthless, and DC cats were just like any other. What Dino also knew was that Gator's concerns drew more from the fact that DC and the Dirty South had just clashed at USP-Coleman in Florida. The possibilities were great that some of those same DC dudes would be on the bus to Death Valley.

Speaking on the issue, Bone said, "Nah Gator, ain't no DC cats on the line. Once they get here, we'll get with them as well. We've all been down long enough to know somebody to holler at. Convicts are going to respect convict rules. If not, they can get the fuck gon' like anybody else. Period."

Although it was a little after 6:30 in the morning, the temperature had risen as the sun began to wash the night away with its bleak rays of light. The gun tower stood like a stone giant, undoubtedly occupied by an officer who was watching their every move. The indoor movement for breakfast was almost over so Dino wanted to conclude the meeting with a few final points.

"Alright, y'all," he said. "What about the economy? Is anyone opposed to keeping the going rate on stamps the same? Or does anyone wanna change it?"

Stamps, which were compound money, were up to seventy-five cents each when bought at commissary. Twenty cost $15.00. The value dropped once used on the compound to $12.00 a book.

"I say keep it where it's at," Jake said.

"Me too," Asian Lee said.

This was the first time he'd spoke but everyone knew his contributions to the compound's economy. He was connected to the Tri-Ad in Asia and their reach gave him access to officers so he supplied almost 90% of the drugs, tobacco, and cell phones they had at the prison.

"Well then," Dino said. "I agree as well. I guess now the only other thing to address is any concerns or issues amongst us."

Tito was a Puerto Rican Latin King out of Connecticut. He was short and stocky in stature with a long ponytail that he kept braided. Taking this moment, he looked to address Jake about a problem he was having.

"I was meaning to get at you," he said to the big man.

"Oh yeah, 'bout what?" Jake asked.

"Biker Dan. He's down with me a grand," Tito said then shrugged his shoulders. "It's been two months now and I'm tired of waiting."

Maniak spoke also, "Dan owes me five hundred. Told me he was waitin' on some money from his people. That was months ago as well."

For a moment, Jake just paused as if in deep thought.

"I'll take care of it," he finally said.

"Anything else?" Dino asked the group.

"Inmates on A and B yards return to your housing units!" the blaring voice of the officer working control echoed off the compound walls.

At that time of the morning, there was no mistaken who he was speaking to. "Well," Dino concluded. "That's it. I appreciate y'all for comin' out."

They all parted ways with mutual respect, heading in the direction of their housing units. Asian Lee, who was on the other side of the fence, sided up to Dino to talk a little business.

"I need you to grab the rest when you have a chance," Lee said under his breath.

Dino understood clearly. "I'll be going back there after ten. I'll see you at lunch."

"That'll be perfect."

As Lee headed to his unit, Dino made his way up the stairs to B3. On his way, he saw Maniak lingering back and speaking with Bone. He knew Bone also had business with Biker Dan and that he owed him. Why he didn't address it was beyond Dino.

Thinking nothing of it, he headed up the steps. He had business to take care of as well. If everything went right, he was going to score big messing with the Asian. With only 2 years left until his release, he needed every penny he could save.

As the meeting between the convicts concluded another meeting was underway inside of the Administration Building...

When Trevor Maddox was promoted from Captain to Assistant Warden, he left USP-Allenwood with the hopes of finally getting his chance to prove himself. He never in a million years thought his opportunity would come so fast. He arrived a little over a year ago. Little did he know that year would bring death to the Warden at that time, Jim Dempster. Since that tragic event, he saw himself go from Assistant Warden to the official Warden, trumping multiple candidates for the same position.

"You're our guy," Washington executives told him at their meeting in DC.

It wasn't that he didn't appreciate the opportunity. He did extremely. It was something more like a feeling deep in his gut. A feeling birthed the day he saw Dempster's head explode right before his eyes. An event spurred by another officer gone rogue. Used up to that point mostly as a training facility for new officers, the prison remained relatively quiet until that day. Hell, it had only been open for 3 years. However, Warden Maddox felt that day was the beginning of bad things to come. To him it felt like an omen.

What a blessing it had been to only have so few inmates. For a USP, the place had seen very few incidents. Most were infractions for disobeying staff, failed drug tests, or sometimes for smoking. Not many knives or stabbings for that matter. Now it seemed Washington was ready to change courses, sending a memo through the regional office that Death Valley would be increasing its population of inmates. All of whom were the black sheep of the FBOP.

Upset that such a drastic move was being made, however, Warden Maddox had no other choice but to comply. His grievances went unheard and now there was no turning back. Now here he was in his conference room standing before a hand full of staff. All of the counselors, case managers, and unit managers sat amongst his lieutenant, captains, and Special Investigation Services department—SIS.

"Good morning ladies and gentleman," he said.

A firm and conditioned man, Warden Maddox stood tall before them. His Irish inherited red hair was neatly parted, giving him a clean and young look. He looked nowhere near the 52 years he actually was.

"Good morning, Warden," came several responses.

Taking a deep breath, he proceeded with the business at hand.

"I called this brief meeting to update you all on our up and coming arrivals here to our prison." Opening his black leather folder, Warden Maddox adjusted his reading glasses. "As I briefed you all at our meeting last week, our population will be increasing, per Washington and Region."

He looked up to see the faces of those before him. He swore he caught an eye or two roll as well as disgusted body language.

"Excuse me, Warden," it was the case manager, James Carson.

"Yes sir," Warden Maddox said, opening the floor.

"When you say increasing, by how much may I ask?"

Warden Maddox knew the ex-marine's mind was clear and sharp. Carson was a young black professional who paid attention to detail. "Over the next sixty days we'll be receiving approximately one thousand inmates."

Carson whistled a sigh of amazement.

Warden Maddox nodded and then said, "It's time. We've been housing now for just over three years. Washington feels we are ready and now we're moving forward."

Mrs. Casey was the unit manager for C-unit. She raised her hand, waiting for the Warden to acknowledge her.

"Sir, what Washington isn't taking into consideration is the level of risk they're putting our officers in," she said, addressing the seriousness of this issue. "The caseloads we're receiving concerning the inmates are of individuals being shipped for disciplinary purposes—"

Warden Maddox raised his hand, cutting her off. "Mrs. Casey, I've addressed this same concern to our regional office in Grand Prairie. Trust me, I have eighteen classified rookies working on this compound. Most are in the units."

"But Warden," Carson interjected. "These inmates are coming from all over. Mostly from the southeast region. Step downs from segregation programs like Security Management Unit, as well as segregated housing units at other facilities. The worst of the worst. What type of position are we realistically putting these rookies, as well as ourselves, in?"

Warden Maddox took his glasses off and said, "Marine, this is a USP. We're all in a hostile position. That's what we trained for. That's what we trained our officers for."

The finality of the Warden's words marinated in each person in the room.

Lt. Frost was the head of SIS and was seated at the table with his fellow staff. Being the driving force behind the facilities conformance, he looked to address the situation.

"There will indeed be a high population of gang members and other high profile individuals. Our segregated compound was built for this. Although your unit teams have profiles, SIS will conduct initial screenings upon bus arrivals to try and capture profiles of individuals we may not have information on. That way we are properly prepared to assess each and every person on that bus."

"So we'll know exactly who we're dealing with," Warden Maddox added. "Look, we knew this day was coming and with it would come much responsibility." Each member of the unit team had no choice but to agree.

"Now," Warden Maddox added. "Captain McDaniels, I want you to make sure we're prepping and getting our officers ready so we can be operating on all cylinders."

Captain McDaniels was ever eager to heed his superiors command. "Yes sir." At 48 years old, he prided himself on being the best the Bureau had ever seen. Running a yard efficiently was his specialty.

As another point of emphasis, Lt. Frost looked to suggest what he felt was important for the unit teams to know. "SIS would like for all officers to have access to each inmates' file. Can they do this from their workstations?"

Pam Cook was the case manager for B-Unit. She and Carson were the only two blacks that held those positions on the yard. "For them to have access wouldn't be difficult. They should have access to department files."

"They do," Carson nodded and said.

Lt. Frost looked at Warden Maddox and said, "This will ensure each officer has complete knowledge of who they're dealing with."

Warden Maddox agreed.

While Lt. Frost was adding his final touches to the up and coming inmate situation...

Ted sat in the parking lot leaned back in his all black Chevy Tahoe. The limo-tinted windows provided the perfect cover as the lieutenant's wife, Nurse Frost, kept her loosely wrapped lips sucking tenderly on his dick. Her tongue danced along his underside as she bobbed from top to the base of his hard meat stick. Ted was in heaven.

"Oooh shit," he hissed as she roughly rolled his nut sack in her right hand.

Nurse Frost looked up at him with her eyes lost in lust. Her mouth was almost as wet as her pussy, which she played with also.

"Yeah," he said, loving the feeling she provided. "Play with that fat pussy girl."

"Mmm-hmmm," was all she could muster.

Their discreet rendezvous fuck sessions began several months prior. It was something neither expected, despite their flirtatious ways. Ted knew fucking the Lieutenant's wife presented many problems, all of which seemed to disappear from his mind the moment he found himself balls deep in her mouth, ass, or pussy.

The veteran nurse tended to his ever growing hard-on like it was a patient in desperate need of attention. With her body angled so that her head fit directly in his lap, she used one hand to widen his thighs to get better access. Then contorting her body even more, she lapped her tongue from beneath his ball sack upward, taking his whole dick into her mouth until she had the full 8 inches down her throat.

"Damn girl," Ted exclaimed.

While she performed her magic, Ted reached his right hand between her legs, sliding three fingers into her sopping wet pussy. As she continued sucking, he got a glimpse of her partially shaven, smooth lips. A blonde fuzzy strip decorated her pussy, most of which was coated in her own juices.

Nurse Frost gave a deep groan of pleasure, signaling her excitement.

"Are you gonna catch all this cum, baby?"

Without missing a beat, she nodded and said, "Mmm-hmm."

"Good," he said, playing with her clitoris faster and faster. " 'Cause it's cumin', baby."

The feeling of his balls tightening caused Ted to slightly raise his hips. He plunged his fingers deep into her pussy as she cupped his balls and sucked his now redheaded monster. Nurse

Frost slurped and lapped her tongue as fast as his fingers fucked her, causing him to shake.

"Here it comes, baby," he told her. "Here it...."

The first spasm rocked him, but the wonderful wife of ten years was not stunned. She continued to drain him of every ounce his body could produce. Ted's dick pumped load after load as he sat there with his eyes rolled into the back of his head. The whole while she kept a vacuumed suction lock on his cock, not allowing a drop to drool out of place.

Nurse Frost ran her freshly manicured nails across his bare thigh, scratching him tenderly. Her tongue was still begging for droplets of cum to coax its tip.

"Damnmit, sugar," he said, pulling his fingers from her twat. They were gooey with her cum, which had shot and poured all over her legs and the truck's seats. "This here honey box gets wetter by the day."

She plopped his now soft dick out of her mouth. "And this dick tastes better each time I suck it."

He loved her dirty mouth. He knew that it was going to be both of their downfall because he just couldn't keep his dick out of it.

Back in B-Unit...

Dino exited his cell just as Carson entered the unit. A few cats pulled up on the case manager, asking various questions about transfers and such. While Dino waited patiently to go work in the back, his partner, Donnie, approached him, pushing a broom inconspicuously.

"You goin' to visit this weekend?"

"Yeah," Dino told him. "My daughter's comin'. Are you goin'?"

"Supposed to," he told him. "Leah is supposed to bring my daughter."

"That's cool. What's up tho'?"

Dino knew his partner had something else on his mind.

Donnie nodded and said, "That money made it. I'm just waitin' on you."

The man was one of a few Dino messed with regarding the business he was involved in. Despite being a certified gang member, Donnie was a hardnosed businessman. His word stayed good and he kept all bullshit far away from him. For this reason, Dino kept him with tobacco, Kush, and whatever else he got his hands on. For him, the hustler was his legs, eyes, and ears.

"Alright, I'll see you with that tonight. Tell your people we got 'em."

"Fa'sho."

By the time he concluded his conversation with Donnie, Dino saw that Carson was finished speaking with the others. Seeing him, the case manager waved Dino over to let him do what he hired him for.

"What's up," Dino greeted him. "You're runnin' late this morning I see."

Carson shook his head, and said, "We had a meeting. Seems that we're getting some buses."

As he spoke, Carson unlocked the side door that led to the back offices.

"I heard," Dino told him.

Carson smiled. "It's crazy how y'all know shit before some of us."

The two of them came to the offices and the first thing Dino smelled was freshly brewed coffee. His counselor, Ms. White, was seated at her desk shuffling through some paperwork. She was a white, elderly woman, who Dino always showed the respectful side of himself because he knew she didn't take no shit.

"Good morning, Ms. White," he said, poking his head into her office.

"Well good morning to you, Patterson."

The sound of high heels clicking came echoing down the hallway. Dino looked up in time to see the other case manager, Ms. Cook, enter. To him, she was the finest woman on the compound. Looking not a day over 30 years old, Ms. Cook stayed dressed professionally, yet always filled out her slacks or skirts with her highly toned physique. With long, permed hair that was always curled or primped, she never let one day go by where she didn't look her best.

"Good morning, Ms. Cook," Dino greeted her.

"Hey there, Dino," she said, calling him by his nickname. "Ms. White, did you put this coffee on?"

"Yes ma'am. I sure did," Ms. White replied.

Ms. Cook went into her office and sat her paperwork on the desk. Then she exited to get a cup of the fresh java.

Carson came out of his office. "Wha'chu wanna knock out first?" he asked Dino.

"I'll do the restrooms first," he told him. "Then I'll hit the staff's bathrooms and mop last. I'll get the offices after lunch."

Unlocking the utility closet for him, Carson left Dino to his tasks.

Grabbing his spray bottles and filling them with Simple Green cleaning solution, Dino filled his mop bucket with fresh water and grabbed two towels. He sat everything by the women's staff bathroom. Then returning to the closet, he got a dust mop and prepared to sweep up the hall and bathrooms.

This was all in preparation.

With a dust mop, Dino made it down the hall and past the offices. He looked to see how engaged the three staff were. They were each in their offices seated at their desks. He continued down the hallway like he routinely did. Then he circled, shook the dust out of the sweeper, and headed back to the utility closet. He went to get Ms. White.

"Could you unlock the bathroom so I can freshen it up?"

With a smile, she rose from her desk, and said, "Sure honey."

Letting her pass, Dino stole a guilty glance at the 50 plus woman's backside. Her hips were wide and her ass was too. He shook his head. Even after ten years, he knew he was wrong for lusting after a woman her age. He wasn't even 40 yet but if he had the chance, he knew he'd no doubt shove his long dick in her.

I've been down too long, he thought shaking his head.

34

Ms. White unlocked the bathroom door and left Dino to do his job. Once he knew she was back in her office, he went to work. The toilets, trash, sink, and mirror wasn't his main concern. No, he had other interests. Taking a quick peek outside the door, he lifted the toilet seat before stepping onto it. Then stretching his arms up he lifted a square in the drop ceiling, removing the corner tile. Knowing he had limited time, Dino fished his hand around until he located what he was looking for.

"Got'cha," he said, finding it.

Once he had a firm grip, he brought what was the last of the package Asian Lee gave him to put up. It was $1,000 worth of tobacco and two ounces of Kush. Wasting no time, Dino stepped down and began tucking the contraband. The tobacco, which was compressed into six small cookie like shapes, went into a back brace he wore like a girdle. He was able to fit the kush in there as well.

He grabbed the spray.

Now it was time for the toilet, sink, and mirror.

2

A few days had passed since the meeting and Big Jake never got the chance to ask Biker Dan about the debts he owed. So that afternoon he made it his business to go to the chow hall and wait for Dan's unit to come in. He knew the weasel dope fiend wouldn't miss a meal. So he patiently sat at the table, picking over nasty sauce poured over partially boiled spaghetti noodles.

"This shit isn't worth my dog eating," Snake said, pushing his tray aside.

Skull was seated next to Jake without a tray.

He nudged the big man. "Here he comes."

Big Jake looked in the direction Skull was looking in and saw Dan standing in line.

Snake and Skull were two Aryan Brothers out of Texas sent to Death Valley for a brutal stabbing they committed at USP-Beaumont. After spending three years in the SHU (Solitary Housing Unit), Region dumped them out in the desert, far away from home as a punishment. They both were in their late 50's with ink slung across their skin older than half the prison's convicts. Lightning bolts, biker chics, and images of the Grim Reaper decorated their white skin. To Big Jake, they were only different in appearance. Other than that, the three of them were functioning on the same wavelength.

Their dials were tuned in on Biker Dan.

The chow hall had sixty tables, which inmates segregated themselves too. Once they came into one of the two entrances, they followed the line to the service bar, retrieving a tray with food, and continuing on for drinks and a seat. Years ago, the federal system earned rave reviews for their food service. Those years were all gone and now the looks on the inmates' faces showed no excitement for the food. Actually, they looked upset.

The whites sat a row behind the Mexicans, who had several tables to themselves. At one time, the whites only had four tables. That was until Big Jake got there. He made it an issue and now they had twice that amount. He knew they'd need more once the buses started rolling in.

Once Biker Dan got his tray and filled a cup with sugar-free Kool-Aid, he made his way to the table. A few cats called out to him from different races. He just tossed a wave their way.

"Later, later," Biker Dan called back to them as he took a seat next to Snake.

Big Jake took a good look at him. "Where you been hidin' at?" he asked almost playfully.

Biker Dan dug into his food, shoveling a fork full of noodles in his mouth. "Well, good afternoon to you too, big guy. Snake, Skull."

The two of them simply nodded.

Biker Dan was around their age, yet scrawny with beady little eyes. On numerous occasions, Big Jake had to speak to him about his financial affairs. Biker Dan liked every drug in the book. If he could shoot it, snort it, or smoke it then it was for him.

"Actually Dan, I came out to ask you why you got Blacks and Mexicans asking me about the money you owe them."

Biker Dan stopped chewing. A disgusted look came across his face. In a low, dramatic tone he said, "If a nigger or dirt back Mexican told you I owe a dime, you tell them I said stand in line."

Big Jake looked back at the little man from Boston and gave a light chuckle. Then with lightning quick speed, he whipped his long arm from under the table, slapping the Be-Jesus out of Biker Dan.

Pow!

Sauce, noodles, and snot flew, splattering Snake's federal issued Khaki shirt. Biker Dan's head snapped to the side, sending his body and ass to fly up out the seat he was in.

"What the—" Biker Dan started to say before he cut himself off.

The commotion caused some of the Mexicans to turn around. For some, they looked a little alarmed and startled by the abrupt aggression. Just as fast as he struck, Big Jake returned to his composed self as Snake roughly helped Biker Dan get back in his seat.

"Now, listen you piece of shit," Big Jake told him calm but firm. "I don't answer shit for you. One week tops. Pay your shit off, understood?"

With one hand up against his already cherry red face, Biker Dan tried his best to make out which of the three Big Jake's he saw was the actual person. "Yea a week.."

Big Jake rose from the table. Snake and Skull followed suit. Without another word said, the three of them made their way to the tray dispensary before exiting the chow hall. Biker Dan sat alone, still dazed by the openhanded wallop he took.

From behind the kitchen's service counter...

Bone was removing the empty four-inch pan of spaghetti noodles from the line. He was line backing for the servers, a job he didn't usually do. He was the head cook but every now and again his supervisor, Mr. Casey, would ask him to help out. With all the money he made out of the kitchen, Bone never told Mr. Casey no.

As he helped keep the food on the line, Bone just happened to see Big Jake slap the shit out of that dope fiend Dan. Bone wanted him whooped but not so bad that he got ran up top to the SHU behind it. Dan owed him too.

Bone's homeboy, Tray, got up from the Crip's table and approached the counter.

"Hey Cuz, you peep that shit?" Tray asked.

He nodded. "Yeah I saw it. Jake checked him about that bread he owin' niggas."

"Cuz, that white boy gotta have that money ASAP! Niggas ain't playin'."

Bone looked to calm his homeboy.

"On 4 Tray, Cuz trust me. If that don't work then Jake is gonna have to take care of it."

Tray seemed pissed. "One of them is gonna. Cuz, that's eight hundred."

As his homeboy walked off, Bone took the empty pan into the back.

The interior of the kitchen was where all of the cooking was done. It was also where the officer's station was located with large refrigerators and freezers to store everything from fruits to frozen meats. Inmates worked in the back either cooking or cleaning everything from the floors to the massive amounts of pans and utensils. A dock was also located at the very back. This is where loads of goods would arrive on a truck.

Once Bone delivered the pan to the scullery area, he saw Maniak standing with Mr. Casey. Maniak's work partner Fats from Louisiana was also there. They worked in the kitchen's warehouse. If Mr. Casey was with them that told Bone that a truck finally came in. He just prayed it was the truck they'd been waiting for.

Maniak saw Bone, gave him a head nod, and then he tore himself from the supervisor.

"Okay, I'll be ready in five minutes. Let me take a piss," Maniak stated then he headed towards the bathroom, and Bone followed.

Standing at the sink, Maniak was washing his hands. Without looking up he said, "Your brother sent that money too."

Bone saw they were indeed alone. "Cool. That nigga be lyin' so much."

"Nah, that nigga just slow. You know he's out there hustlin'."

Despite being opposite sides of gang life, they both had a lot of love for each other. Bone and Maniak did five years in California Youth Authority. Much respect existed between them. Maniak's love for Bone remained and now they were getting money together.

Maniak had him plugged in. "So listen," he started to say quick and in a whisper, slightly louder than the hiss of the running water. "We're about to go snatch this shit now. Tell yo' people to get that money to my people if they wanna eat."

"Fa'sho."

"As for the work, it'll be in the same place. Get'cho ass in and out as fast as you can. Remember, red x and one bag."

There was no more that needed to be said. This was simply routine for him.

When Maniak left out, Bone exited soon afterwards. His senses were heightened by the fact that shit was finally about to go down. For the past 4 months, they'd been running a smooth operation getting tobacco, cell phones, ecstasy, crystal meth, and kush in through the kitchen. Maniak figured out a way to get it in when he realized all the products came from a certain company. He brought the idea to Dino, and the Asians were brought in to make it happen. Lee's people perfected duplicating the company's label and packaging then Wa-lah! The shit actually came: two pounds of tobacco, eight ounces of kush, two cell phones, four and a half ounces of crystal, and two hundred pills of ecstasy.

From that point forward, the compound came alive.

Now that they received word that their numbers were increasing, Dino really wanted to double that amount. Dudes like Bone got a fee for his role, which was enough to pay for help. If he wished to purchase whatever he'd like he was able to at a low-low price. So this is how he included his Crip homeboys to make sure they ate as well.

Ty and Lil' B were two cats from New York who worked as kitchen orderlies. They were really two scammers who only acted like they were working so they could get close to the food and steal. Bone caught them both standing by the bakery talking to one of the workers through the door.

"I need five pounds tonight," Ty was saying.

The guy they were speaking to was a Paisa Mexican. "Si, Si, at dinner."

Lil' B turned from the door. "Man, if they didn't keep this door locked, I'd be runnin' sugar out this bitch left and right."

Pure sugar was like crystal meth or crack cocaine on prison compounds. Manufacturing homemade alcohol was its main use. So Lil' B and Ty kept the white boys with it and in return they'd receive multiple bottles of white lightning. The shit was potent enough to light on fire.

Bone looked to pull them up on more serious business, and said, "Look, the truck is here."

Despite their hustling ways, these two cats were loyal and Bone knew it. They wouldn't give their mom a plug if it meant taking food out of their mouths. Because of this, he paid them an ounce of kush for each run and that is something they loved indeed.

So without saying a word, they went to the utility closet and grabbed a push broom and mop. To make it look good, they went to work. Meanwhile, Bone went to one of the large cook pots and lifted its lid. Maniak, Fats, and Mr. Casey had long gone to the dock to unload the truck. He knew they'd be rolling the carts in at any moment.

Right on cue, the squeak of the cart's wheels could be heard from around the corner. "I'm tellin' you, Peyton Manning is still the best quarterback in the league," Mr. Casey was saying.

The obese white man wasn't really believing his point.

Fats shook his head, and said, "The man is almost fifty! He's been in the league since the late nineties. He need to retire again!"

Mr. Casey stopped his big butt waddled walk. "Don't y'all still got Drew Brees?" he asked.

Maniak was pulling the cart as he listened to them debate. Once they came to the warehouse door, Mr. Casey took his keys from the hook on his belt and unlocked it. Fats opened the door as Maniak steered the cart filled with bags, cans, and boxes. Mr. Casey made up the rear, letting the door close slightly behind them.

Bone nodded to both Ty and Lil' B, and they nodded back.

About two minutes passed before Maniak, Fats, and the supervisor came out. Bone knew the routine. This was just one trip out of at least three more. In between each trip, Mr. Casey never locked the warehouse door. As soon as they exited, Bone waited until they rounded the corner to the dock before he made his way into the warehouse. He was like a cat burglar at night.

Once inside, Bone headed past several rows of racks; boxes of everything from spices to cereal filled the shelves. Fifty pound bags of sugar, flour, hot cereal, and other dry products sat in bulk. Knowing he didn't have much time, he jogged down the back aisle to where the back freezer was located. He opened the door and went in, catching a cool blast of air. Then he closed the door, keeping it opened just a peek.

Squeaking wheels...

"Y'all haven't won a Super Bowl since Hurricane Katrina," Mr. Casey could be heard shooting shots at Fats.

"And y'all still try'na get another one in Denver!" Fats shot back.

Bone listened on until he heard them leave out again. Once he was sure, he came out and ran down the aisle where he knew the bag would be. It was a large Quaker Oats oatmeal bag. At first, he passed the aisle but he doubled back and found it.

He heard voices.

"John Elway is about ready ta' come quarterback again." It was Fats still on Mr. Casey's Denver Broncos.

Bone flinched, damn near running into the shelf, trying to run back into the freezer.

"Don't you speak blasphemy! John could never replace Peyton," Mr. Casey stated, as he looked appalled by just the thought.

"So, you sayin' Manning is better than Elway?"

"It's a fact!" the supervisor stated.

Bone watched as Fats and Maniak unloaded the cart. Once they finished, they headed back out.

Coming out the freezer, he knew this was his last shot. Heading back to the oatmeal aisle, Bone moved fast.

"Where you at? Where in the fuck—" He cursed as he looked through the bags, turning them on their side and about.

Then he saw it.

The Red X.

"Come here bitch."

As if it was a drunk woman, Bone tossed the bag over his right shoulder. He knew time was of the essence so he moved like he was rushing out of a burning house.

Now the scary part about all of this was once he came out of the warehouse door anything could happen. Anyone could be standing there. The Warden himself could be there. Him holding that bag would not only get him busted, but it would also raise suspicion. That was a chance he had to take. So with nuts of steel, he cracked the door, peeked, and then took off with the bag right out in the open.

Ty was the first to meet him. "Here," he said, taking the bag.

"I'd bet you five hundred right now y'all don't beat us by nobody's ten points," the sound of Mr. Casey's voice caused Ty's eyes to grow big as saucers.

Lil' B was posted next to the big pot Bone opened the lid to. So keeping his eyes forward, Ty kept in that direction. Luckily, Mr. Casey was so wrapped up in wanting to bet that he was blind to an inmate carrying a fifty-pound bag of oatmeal, Kush, cell phones, tobacco, and meth.

When Bone saw Maniak and Maniak saw Ty, all of their hearts stopped.

"Hey, you!" Mr.Casey yelled.

Everybody froze.

Ty had just made it to the pot. Still, with his back turned, he eased the bag out of his hands, into the large bowl of the pot, and then he turned around.

Mr. Casey said, "Yeah you." He pointed around the floor area. "Mop up all this access water. It's no time to stand around. Let's get some work done."

Bone took a deep breath.

"Yes, sir," Ty said.

"And you too!" Mr. Casey shouted and pointed towards Lil' B.

Lil' B saluted the man and grabbed his mop stick.

Mr. Casey opened the warehouse door and turned his attention back to Fats. "And don't think I wouldn't take that bet."

"You'd be five hundred dollars broker," Fats replied.

As Maniak wheeled the cart, he took a quick glance at Bone who gave him the thumbs up.

Down the corridor in the Officers Mess Hall...

Leon, Ted, and Hal sat at one of the small tables enjoying a lunch break. All three partners had been working various jobs on the compound. This gave them an opportunity to meet up every afternoon. This was their last day because the quarter was about to change and new posts would be assigned to them.

Hal was just venting about how he and his wife weren't having sex as often and Leon thought to lend him some advice.

"Listen, do you really want her to kick things back in gear?"

Hal nodded his head, and said, "I mean-Fuckin' right."

"Okay, trust me this always get women wetter than a water slide."

Hal was all ears. Anything that would help him, he was more than open to. "What's that?" Hal asked.

"This big black dick," Leon said with a straight face. "Call me, I'll come by, and I promise you I'll get her ass back in gear in no time."

Ted started laughing.

"Fuck you," was all Hal could say, falling for Leon's bullshit. "And what are you laughing at?"

Ted shrugged, and said, "Don't go at me. You always come for me whenever he gets on you."

The door to the OM opened up, causing them to look in that direction. Nurse Frost entered wearing some tight scrubs. With a nasty walk, she switched up to the counter. She made no attempt to hide her intense stare Ted's way.

Leon nudged him underneath the table. "Boy, if the LT finds out you're fucking his wife—"

"What's he gonna do?" Hal asked. "Shit, from what I've heard, she's ran through several compounds in the BOP. He probably knows."

Ted shrugged it off, while keeping his eyes glued to her bouncing backside. He didn't give a fuck about the lieutenant. "He's not gonna find out shit," Ted said before taking a sip of his soda. "Plus, it's not like I'm on her. She's stalkin' me. I'm just being polite about it."

"Well, that's mighty nice of you," Leon acknowledged. "To deny her your pink dick would be cruel and unjust."

"Now wouldn't it," Ted smiled, and said.

At that moment, the door opened again and in walked two female rookies, and one was Alexis Green. To Leon, she was a goddess in the flesh at 5'7," 160 pounds max, with smooth dark skin, short styled hair, and an ass and pair of thighs a plastic surgeon couldn't duplicate. When she entered, her uniform khaki pants were snatched up and creased perfectly between her thighs, giving her pussy lips an outline a camel in Dubai would fall in love with.

Leon couldn't help but to stare.

The other girl was Erin Jiminez. She was a beautiful Mexican chick, petite with long flowing curly hair. She had a nice little tight ass, but her best asset was her exotic hazel eyes. Both girls were in their mid-twenties.

"Hey guys," Erin called to them.

"What's up, y'all," Leon said in his casual way.

"Just chillin'," came Alexis. "Takin' a break."

Erin saw Nurse Frost and with her arms spread wide she greeted her with a hug. "Heeeeey!"

Nurse Frost smiled, accepting her in a small embrace. Ted couldn't help but smile. Leon knew it was because Ted fantasized about fucking them both. Hal just shook his head.

"Hey there, Lexi," Nurse Frost said.

"Lexi?" Leon asked with eyebrows raised.

Alexis looked at him as he was obviously flirting. "It's Ms. Green to you," she said, and then she gave him a crooked smile.

He surrendered with his hands raised high.

"Whatever you want."

Alexis smiled, and stated, "You learn quick and I like that."

Nurse Frost nonchalantly extended her hand, and said, "Officer Gibbs, Shiver."

Ted and Hal shook her hand. Leon noted the spark between Ted and Nurse Frost.

The girls concluded their meet and greet with the boys and found a table together. Leon's eyes were glued to Ms. Green's ass. It was fully proportioned, cut, and round like a baby donkey's butt. Their eyes locked for a minute as she looked back over her shoulder.

"I got a hundred I tap that," Leon said to his crew.

Hal looked at Ted, and asked, "Did he say a hundred?"

Ted nodded. "Yep."

"Sixty days," Hal said, setting a time limit.

Leon smiled. "I'ma at least need ninety. By then she'll be callin' me daddy in front of Warden Maddox."

"Bet!" Hal couldn't resist.

"You want in on this?" Leon looked at Ted and asked.

"You still owe me from the nurse," Ted said, head gesturing where the girls sat.

"So bet back double," Leon suggested. "Come on, give me some action."

Ted smiled while taking a sip of his drink. "Okay, I'm in."

At the girls' table...

Nurse Frost was checking up on the rookie officers. She knew Erin because the girl's cousin Paul worked with both her and her husband at several prisons. This was the reason the girl sought a career in corrections. The other rookie, Alexis, was the newest and neither had been there over 9 months.

"So how's it coming girls?" Nurse Frost asked.

Alexis was the first to respond. "I am glad the quarter changed."

"Oh, where they puttin' you?" Erin asked, as if she'd been meaning to.

"Out of this corridor. I finally got my first unit," Alexis said proudly.

Nurse Frost looked at both of them. "Y'all haven't worked a unit yet?"

"Not a whole quarter," Erin replied.

"Yeah," came Alexis. "We only trained at thirty day posts."

"Do you like workin' them?" Erin crinkled her nose and asked.

"Shit, I don't mind. Them mutha'fuckas don't scare me," Alexis spoke with extreme confidence and swagger.

"Do you feel threatened?" Nurse Frost asked Erin.

Erin shook her head. "No, not like that. I'm just having a hard time getting used to seeing a lot of stuff is all."

Nurse Frost smiled, and said, "Yeah, you run into a lot working those units."

"Who you telling," Alexis said. "I was countin' on a double shift last week. As soon as I came to this one cell, the guy inside was standing in the middle of it masturbating."

Erin's nose crinkled again, and she said, "Yeah, that type of stuff."

"But you don't get it," Alexis continued. "The mutha'fucka was holding at least eleven inches in his hand. The shit scared me."

"Made you wanna cross your legs?" Nurse Frost asked.

"Sew that bitch shut!" Alexis exclaimed.

Nurse Frost laughed. She was so caught up in her conversation she almost missed Ted staring right at her.

"So what unit you gonna be working?" Erin asked her friend. "They got me in visitation."

"I'ma be in B-Unit…"

As Alexis explained, the nurse slid a hand beneath the table and in between her legs. Her clit was hard and her pussy

47

was getting wet. Ted turned her on with his crew cut and care-freestyle. She wished she could get him to come up to medical after work. One of the empty rooms would do them just find and the thought of him sliding his thick dick into her from the doggy style position made her pussy jump.

"Hey honey!" The voice of her husband made the nurse flinch in her seat. When she looked up, she saw his face, all smiles.

"Oh, hey... uhh..."

"Richard... Richard Frost. I'm your husband." The lieutenant smiled as if making a joke.

Nurse Frost smiled. "Hey baby, where you comin' from?"

Lt. Frost bent and kissed her. "Hey officers," he said to both Alexis and Erin.

"Hey Lieu."

Frost turned back to his wife. "I was up at the Cap's office. Gotta head out to Blythe later." The city of Blythe was over 30 minutes away.

"For what?"

"Pick up an inmate from their county. I'll probably be gon' two to three hours," he explained. "So I wanted to come let 'chu know."

She smiled. "Well okay babe. If you're not back I'll just see you at the house."

"Okay babe," he said leaving out.

Once gone, Nurse Frost looked in the direction of Ted and smiled. With her husband gone she could play. She wondered the odds of Ted denying her a quick visit up at medical.

Oh, he'll come, she thought smiling. *I'll make sure of it.*

3

The idea Maniak and Dino masterminded turned out to be ingenious. Bringing Asian Lee on board took the operation to another level. They were getting in whatever they wished for. However, each step had to be executed properly because one slip could cost them the whole hook up.

Both Dino and Maniak took pride in figuring out every aspect of their plan to get and store everything that came in. Once the package was retrieved from the kitchen's warehouse, it was then transported to the scullery, located in the dining hall area. From there, it would be broken down. Lee's people compressed all tobacco and marijuana, while also tightly packaging whatever else came in. Bones job would be to assure only his crew would be in the dishwashing area. They would then bust everything up before putting it in a large hot trash bin; a sensitive material trash bucket.

Aside from working as an orderly in his unit, Dino also worked part time for the compound. This gave him the freedom to roam around. Once the contraband was in the hot trash bin, Dino would retrieve it when he did his rounds. Of course, an officer accompanied him but Dino's relationship with all the compound officers was cool. Once the drop was ready, he pulled off the mission with no hassle. Officer Taylor thought nothing as they talked about fine ass celebrity women they'd love to fuck. From there, Dino's only concern was getting his prized possession into his unit.

The transfer to the unit was a clever one, yet simple. Dino would time his rounds so that once the recreation move was called for incoming/outgoing inmates he'd be parked in front of his unit. The large trash cart he pushed helped to block plenty of the view, so when his mules came down the steps he'd hand them the pillow cases filled with everything and they'd haul it upstairs to his young Piru partner, Donnie.

Never had it failed.

Neither did it.

Letting a few days pass, Dino laid low to throw off any wanna-be lookie-loo dudes in his unit. He knew SIS kept paid informants inside every unit. They were the cameras that walked and dressed in khaki. So once he stashed each bundle in the unit's team staff bathroom, he got with Lee to let him know it was all good. Then when he found the right moment he broke out the first batch to distribute amongst those who helped make it possible.

Dino and his partner Donnie were up in the cell. The specific bundle he grabbed had ½ pound of tobacco, ¼ pound of kush, and 56 grams of crystal meth. For two hours straight they measured and sacked up each so Dino could get shit moving. He already sent out two mules to deliver Lee's issue to C-Unit. Now Dino was taking care of the others who'd sent money.

"Okay, I need you to stash these," he said to Donnie.

Eighteen zip locked sandwich bags sat on Dino's bed. Donnie began stuffing them in the three variety oatmeal boxes he'd bought. "I'll keep the Buglar separated from the green."

"Cool."

The sound of keys jingling caused them both to pause.

"Take a look," Dino told his partner.

Making his way to the cell's door, Donnie was caught off guard when all of a sudden it came open. He came face to face with Ms. Green. She was working their block for the new quarter. "Uhm… can y'all step out… shake down."

Dino saw the female officer and recognized her. "Hey Ms. Green," he said trying to not look suspicious.

Donnie stepped aside, then back towards the bunk. Nonchalantly he picked up the boxes and closed them.

"How you doin' Patterson," she replied.

Dino shrugged. "I'm just helpin' my homeboy out with something to eat."

With her eyes searching as she spoke she said, "Well if you're finished... just give me a few minutes and I'll be out of your way."

"Sure thing." Dino knew she was really cool. But because she was new, young and thick in the hips, she drew a lot of attention. Ever since she started working their unit she'd been shaking down cells and even wrote a guy an incident report when she caught him staring at her ass.

Donnie was the first to step out. Dino was behind him. Once they were both out of the cell, she dropped one of Dino's towels over the small window and closed the door.

"You ain't leave nothing did you?"

Dino shook his head. "Nope, you got it all." With that being said Donnie marched off with the oatmeal boxes towards his cell.

Dino stayed downstairs in his unit. He had a good shot of the unit's front door and a few televisions. It was a little after 6 p.m. and there were guys seated on the open floor, chairs positioned in front of several televisions. While his cell was searched, he waited patiently.

"Yo, Dee."

The only person who called him Dee was a cat he got along with named Slim. "What's up man," he said giving the tall man some dap.

Slim was a cool dude out of Los Angeles who had been down since his early 20's. He was now 45 still hopeful that one day his life sentence would be overturned. "Baby up in your shit, huh?" he asked towering over Dino.

He nodded. "Yeah."

Slim shook his head. "Why she be trippin' so hard?"

"You know how they be when they first start working. She's just trying to prove herself."

"Yeah, she's still on her year probation."

Dino knew Slim didn't come to talk about the C.O. "So what's on your mind?"

Slim smiled. "You remember that website you helped me write a bio for? The one to meet women?"

"Caring for convicts.com? Yeah, why, did you get on it?"

"Yep. And guess what? I got a hit already." Slim was excited.

Dino knew that Slim was a good person. "Oh yeah," he said equally happy. "She got at 'chu already?"

"Yep. She asked me to send a visiting form and everything."

"Already? Damn that was fast. Have you even spoken to her yet?" he asked.

Slim popped his collar jokingly. "Man, that's all we've been doing. In her letter she said she loved my introduction letter, so she sent her number and fifty bucks so I could call."

"What?"

"Yep. I just wanted to tell you thanks man."

Dino waved him off. "Man it's nothing. Anytime you—" He paused when he saw the officer open his cell door and wave him over. "Excuse me, Slim." His thoughts ran wild.

Did I leave something?

As soon as Dino made it to his door, Ms. Green was still standing inside the cell with one hand on her thick hip and the other holding a large manila envelope. "What's this?"

Taking a deep breath, Dino was almost at a loss for words. Inside the envelope held a contraband item, he felt embarrassed by. It was a full penetration colored, nude magazine called wet candy. "Uhh," he dropped his head. "I tried to keep that tucked."

"Well it wasn't tucked good enough." She tossed it on his bunk. "Peterson, I'ma give you a break this time. Anyway, I know you are good with a lot of these guys in the unit. Just pass the word around… don't fuck with me and I won't fuck with y'all program."

He understood. "I got 'chu Ms. Green."

She walked past him and then before exiting she said, "WET CANDY?"

He dropped his head again. "Please, don't judge me."

"I'd be the last person qualified to do that," she laughed.

Something about her statement made Dino wonder what she meant.

The door opened.

"What's up? You cool?" It was Donnie.

"Yeah, I'm straight."

"I thought you was up in here getting some head or something," he said.

Dino shook his head. "I wish."

In A-Unit...

Big Jake stood in the cell of Snake and Skull while the two tested the crystal meth he just got from Asian Lee. Both took turns sharing the hypodermic needle they came up on from medical. After Skull finished, he looked at Snake, who was already feeling the effects.

"Good," Snake confirmed.

Skull agreed. "What's he askin'?"

"Same price," Jake told them.

Snake wasn't pleased. "Three hundred a gram is highway robbery. He's fuckin' stickin' it to us and showing those fuckin' niggers all the love."

Big Jake wasn't into using drugs. His only concern was the money. Snake's comment about Lee was absolutely correct. It seemed the Asian wouldn't come down on the prices for him either, although he spent thousands at a time. "Yeah, I'm gonna talk to him about that. In the meantime, how long until that lightning is ready?"

Skull reached over and opened the bottom locker. Inside sat a swollen bag wrapped with a blanket. "Tomorrow morning I'm shinin' this shit off."

The big man seemed pleased. The hard liquor was his only indulgence. "Save me four bottles."

"We got'chu brother."

"Hey," Snake looked up at Jake with erratic eyes jumping in their sockets. The meth was obviously taking a hold of him. "What's up with the cigarettes?"

Big Jake opened the cell door. "Get that lightning bottled up and I'll have something for ya."

The unit was alive as people mingled about. The officer working was a fat fucker who kept his ass parked in his office's chair, probably surfing the net for porn. Jake saw him engaged and made his way over to the Asians' section to have a discussion with Lee.

A hustler and serious businessman, Lee was seated at a table inside the common area of the unit. He was handling some business involving the gambling ticket he ran. Lee's "Vegas Sports" ticket was the only one on the compound and it seemed to Jake everyone in their unit was gunning at the Asians' riches.

A gambler looking to try his luck was standing next to Lee. "So how much is Green Bay giving the Forty Niners?"

Lee looked at his master sheet. "It's Green Bay minus three."

"Okay, give me Green Bay," the gambler said. "That'll make four picks. Put twenty dollars on my freeze out."

Lee wrote down the bet. "Okay, got'chu."

Once the business was done, Big Jake stepped to Lee. "I need to speak to you."

The Asian got up. "Hey Jay, as soon as the game kicks off all bets are closed."

The other Asian, Jay, nodded. "Alright." Then he turned back to the television set.

Jake followed Lee to his cell. Pulling the door closed behind him, the big fella looked to see if he could get some understanding with the man. "My people said the meth is good."

Lee nodded, raising his palms while shrugging his shoulders. "Hey, I told you. My people always send the best."

Jake leaned against the wall and folded his arms. "Listen, you and I both know this compound increasing is going to bring more money."

"Of course."

"And so I'm looking to increase my buy. But I'm going to need a better deal."

Lee looked at Jake and shook his head. "It depends on how much of an increase you're talking about. I feel that the prices we're doing now is more than fair."

"Come on Lee, you're givin' me grams for two-fifty and I'm buying ten at a time," Jake said in all seriousness.

"And that's saving you five hundred," Lee continued. "I know the goin' price is three. Sometimes three-fifty."

"Well what if I go up to twenty grams."

The idea caused Lee to really think about it. Finally, he said, "Listen, I'll give you the whole twenty-eight grams for fifty-six hundred. That's a whole ounce. You can turn around and make a grand sellin' it wholesale."

Jake liked the numbers but he felt like the Asian could do better. "Well, at least that's a start. What about the tobacco? We're already at eight hundred a can. I wanna buy ten at six. Can you work that for me?"

Lee wasn't happy about his request. "You're asking a lot Jake. I mean, I could just sit on it and get every penny."

The idea that Lee wouldn't bend for him changed Jake's demeanor. He came off the wall, standing tall and firm. "So let me get this straight," he said slow and clear so he could get some understanding. "This little pact you got with the Blacks... there's no room for any love for the whites?"

Lee shook his head and laughed. "Who are you to question me about my business Jake? Black, white... all I see is green. But if so, what of it?"

Jake's first thought was to rush the little man, grab him by the throat and choke him to death. Instead, he just nodded his head. "Okay, so that's how it's gonna be?"

"You're making this more complicated than it should be," Lee said. "I've been more than fair. Look, fifty-six for the ounce and I'll do six-fifty per can, if you're gonna get ten of 'em. Jake, that's the best I can do."

Although he wasn't satisfied, Jake decided to mask his frustrations. Going ahead with the numbers, he got the information as to where he needed to send the money. However, he promised himself down the road he'd muscle Lee out of the picture. One way or the other.

Once he made it back to Snake and Skull's cell, Jake found both men tweaking the fuck out. Skull was fiddling with an old Koby radio. He had it unscrewed and busted open with its insides sprawled all over the lower bunk. Snake, on the other hand, was inside his locker fucking with the batch of hooch.

"I promise," he said startling the two upon his entrance. "Shits gonna change around here for the whites. Even if somebody gotta die."

Without looking up from his tinkering, Skull said, "I'm wit'chu brother."

With that, Jake allowed himself to get lost in his own thoughts.

Many things were unfolding within the walls concrete compound. From the warden trying to prepare his officers for the upcoming transition of inmates, to his officers handling life as correctional officers how they saw fit. A world existed between inmates centered around a code of politics, motivated by money, drugs and power. With all combined, it brought a community of life in the most unlikely place.

The Desert of California.

For days, Dino maneuvered tobacco and drugs onto the prison's compound. Him and Lee's relationship wasn't something people knew much about. Only a few knew to make the connection. Lee had his people and Dino had his. Whenever they needed to pass messages they did so discreetly. The same with their supply. Dino took care of the blacks mostly, and Lee took care of the others. Together they touched just about every car on the yard, from hustlers to addicts. In the end, everyone was basically happy, or so it seemed.

Word of the buses rolling in brought awareness to the fact that the prison was up for a change; most gripped about the increase. For the most part, the 350 there ate good and liked the peace and quiet; 98% percent of them all had their own cells. Out of the twelve units, only four were open and those were partials. More inmates meant other units would be opened and the idea of that brought the mental image of congestion. It was a reality they knew they'd have to face one day. A day that was drawing near.

In the meantime, Dino continued on his grind. His time in prison was almost up and in less than 24 months, he planned to be vacationing in Cancun, sipping Pina Coladas. He felt this operation with the Asian was his opportunity to make that vacation, and more, possible. All he had to do was keep his affairs in order and the money would stack itself.

The day of the meeting, Gordo had a doctor's appointment and couldn't be present. Dino hadn't found time to speak with him because of the shipment landing. So when he got word the Paisa's shot caller wanted to see him, he set aside some time to see the man.

Once dinner concluded and night yard was called, Dino stepped out alone. It was peaceful out. The desert sky was clear of any clouds and the temperature was around 78 degrees, despite it being a little after seven. There were maybe 90 people out; some shooting basketball, a few playing handball and others walking or hanging on their respective yards. Dino scanned the fence to see if he saw his friend already out there. Being that the Mexican stayed on C-Yard, he had to post up by that fence to speak with him.

Making his way in that direction, Dino saw Gordo and his right hand man, as they walked towards the fence. Dino really liked doing business with the Mexican. To him, Paisas were more serious about the worth of money. Still rooted in Mexico, they knew the hardships of living. Unlike Americans, they'd live meager just to stack for a major come up. He learned a lot from doing business with them and the Asians. He knew by fucking with them he'd pick up traits that could make him rich.

"Buenos Noches, Dino," Gordo said with a friendly smile.

Dino nodded. "Yes it is," he replied. Despite the friendliness of the Mexican, he knew that Gordo was a cold-blooded killer. A high-ranking member of the Sinaloa Cartel, he was labeled ruthless. However, Dino found that as long as he kept his business and word good, then everything else would reflect that.

"I've been trying to catch up with you, my friend." Gordo stepped to the fence while his partner stayed off to the side.

Dino joined him. "I apologize. But things have gotten a little busy for me."

Gordo nodded. "I've heard but let's talk about the meeting first. My people speak of buses."

"Yeah, the word is we're getting close to a thousand new cats," he explained. "We just wanted to touch basis... you know, let our people know about the hands off policy; school them to our rules here at DV."

"Okay. Let everyone on your side of the yard know I agree. The Paisas will be... how do you say, orientated when they arrive. I guess we'll be getting our share."

Dino laughed. "Oh, I'm sure." He knew Paisas made up a nice portion of the federal population because of their violation of re-entry laws. "Also," he continued. "We discussed any issues that existed between our cars."

"Were there any between anyone and my people?" Gordo asked.

"Not that I know of. How about with the Blacks? Are there any issues with us and your people?"

Gordo shook his head. "No, not at all."

"Good."

Looking to get to other business Gordo said, "So, give me some good news. Are you ready for me yet?"

The last time he dealt with Gordo, Dino was asked about cellphone prices. When he gave Gordo a price of $2,000 the man asked immediately for the person he needed to send the money to. Dino convinced him to wait until he got the phones in. Well, now he had it and it was time to get two-grand richer.

Shoving his hands into his pants' pocket, Dino looked up at the gun tower and nonchalantly kicked a rock. "Yep, I got it. Brand new with internet access. The works."

Gordo couldn't control his excitement.

"And the name to who you want the money sent?"

Dino removed his hands from his pocket. A small white piece of paper was in his left hand as he passed the info through the fence. "My daughter. As soon as she confirms it, I'll send word when to meet me. Please make sure nobody…"

Gordo stopped him. "Your family's information is safe with me."

"I appreciate that."

"I also wanted to ask about that other thing," Gordo said. "The cigarettes and mota."

Dino looked up to the tower and then turned his back to it. "Yeah, I'm ready for that too. How much?"

"I don't know. I'm thinking enough to put up, especially if we're getting more people. I figure a couple grand worth."

Dino and the man discussed the particulars. The cans of tobacco would go for $650 and the kush at $1,500 an ounce. Dino didn't mind working him the deal since he was spending so much. With the phone included, Gordo's tab came to $4,800; money Dino would have put up for when he got out.

From an overhead view, the box shaped prison sat boldly on dry land. Geographically it was built 24 miles from Interstate-15 so those traveling from LA to Las Vegas wouldn't see or even know it was out there.

The small road off I-15 was so nondescript that the few commuters traveling with the all-white bus didn't see it exit. The FBOP transportation was being handled by Death Valley officers who picked up the convicts from the airbase in Adelanto, C.A. All hard nose criminals. The beginning of the many buses expected to come.

The time was high noon and the sun burned the desert land unforgivingly. The A/C was on and cool air blew inside the 40 passenger school-styled bus. The tint on the windows shielded the blazing glare as criminals of every race sat shackled wrist, waist, and ankles. One officer sat in a cage of the bus' rear. Armed with a double barrel shot gun, the C.O. watched with a keen eye as the group grew loud, obnoxious, and obscene.

Joe-Joe was sitting in his seat next to the window. He was shackled to his other homeboy from DC named Weezy. Both had long dreadlocks, dark skin, and the marks of hard felons. Transferred to USP-DV from the riot they had at USP-Coleman, Joe-Joe awaited his arrival to the new prison.

"Fuck that Mo', Weezy called to another one of their homeboys named Champ. "If the bitch ain't suckin', I ain't fuckin'."

Champ was a large, bald headed man around 45 years old. He was an original convict of Lorton State Prison, until the inmates of that prison were transferred over the FBOP. The name Champ came from his years of winning boxing competitions while at Lorton. His hands were vicious as his attitude. "You fakin', slim. I got'chu buying a bitch a bag before you get top or bottom."

Joe-Joe laughed. He knew Champ loved the jokes.

Out of the inmates, there were six on board from DC. Joe-Joe had the most influence and Champ was the most feared, but each one of them were dangerous. Petey Moe was another who'd been down over 15 years. A career criminal, he looked forward to being out on the West Coast, even if it was the desert.

Tired of the long ass drive, Petey Moe turned in his seat and asked the officer in the cage, "How much more until we get there?"

With a stone cold face, the officer looked through his dark tinted Oakley shades. "Why? You got somewhere to be?"

"Man fuck you, cracka ass pig," he responded aggressively. "I gotta be up in ya bitch, that's where I gotta be."

Weezy, Joe-Joe, and Champ were all now focused on the interaction between their homeboy and the officer.

"Turn your ass back in that seat, tough guy."

But Petey Moe wouldn't be intimidated. "Why don't you come out that cage and turn me around?"

At the front of the bus, seated behind the driver ,was Lieutenant Frost. "Keep it down back there. We'll be there soon."

Petey Moe was still focused on the officer in the cage. "Punk bitch," he said turning back in his seat.

It took 15 minutes from the time they exited to arrive at the prison. After passing the guard's shack, the bus entered into the walls, rounding towards the classification section of Receiving and Discharge. There, the prisoners were unloaded, counted and led in shackles inside of R and D where they were placed into holding cells.

Joe-Joe sat on the concrete bench next to Weezy. Petey Moe was in the cell as well. About twelve others accompanied them as officers began filing other convicts into another cell.

"I'm movin' as fast as I can," Champ barked.

Joe-Joe and his homeboys turned their attention towards the window. Champ was being harassed by the same C.O. who held the shot gun in the cage of the bus.

"Pull up your fuckin' pants," the officer told him.

"Why don't chu pull'em up for me," Champ responded. He stopped walking altogether, tired of the police's shit.

Several other officers worked the process of herding in the inmates so the commotion drew attention.

"You keep movin' or I'll move your ass myself," the officer said. His face turning beet red.

Looking the man square in his eyes, Champ's reflexes kicked in. With his arms in restraints and ankles shackled, he thrust his forehead right into the bridge of the officer's nose.

"Ahh!" The blow made the officer stumble backwards. His hands shot to his nose as blood sprayed through his fingers. Joe-Joe, Weezy, and Petey Moe were behind the glass rooting Champ on.

"Kill that bitch!"

"That's right, Champ!"

On cue, the other officers sprang into action. Six to eight of them rushed and tackled Champ. Without the support of his hands, his body took a violent crash, headfirst.

"Pussy mutha'fuckas!" he yelled as knees and elbows pinned him to the floor.

"Get those inmates into the cell!" an officer commanded another.

Squirming aggressively, Champ saw the C.O. he was arguing with. He was above him, with an elbow to the back of his neck. The officer was only inches away from Champ's face, blood still pouring from his nose.

"Thewwww!!!"

The thick wad of saliva spit across the officer's face, into his mouth and eyes.

"Get his ass!" the officers rallied.

From the cell's window, his homeboys watched in dismay as Champ got his ass whooped. The officers turned brutal, plummeting and stomping him with their combat boots. Then once they came to their senses, they called medical before taking him to the SHU.

This was the 2nd sign that things were going to be different.

THE WALL

EPISODE 2
BREAKING THE JOINT IN

1

B iker Dan sat in his cell alone. A towel was draped over the door to block the window so he would have some privacy. He was at the desk eagerly preparing his daily dose of meth. The soda can cooker, water, cotton, and syringe were all lined up. After placing a nice amount of the half-gram he'd bought onto the cup of the can's bottom, Dan cut a strip of foil to prepare a light. Then he placed a few drops of water onto the can.

That's when a knock came to his door.

"Hey yo, Dan. Are ya shittin'?" It was his cellmate, Carl.

Dan knew he didn't want nothing. He was just checking to see if he was missing out on a free high. "Yeah, you asshole."

"Well I need my water bottle," he cried. "I'm try'nah go out on the move."

"They got water outside!" he barked.

With disgust, his cellie walked off with a huff and a puff.

Now back to business.

Dan rolled a wick out of tissue and using a battery he lit it with the foil. Once he got a good blaze going, he picked up the cooker and mixed the solution until the water grew cloudy. Once he got it there, he extinguished the flame in the toilet, used the cotton, and filled the syringe.

He licked his lips. Then flexing his hand he worked up his veins. "Come to daddy."

Dan popped his skin and entered a good vein. He drew back on the syringe's plunger and a stream of blood signaled he was in a main line. With his mouth watering, he plunged slowly, draining the methamphetamine into his system. Instantly, a tingling sensation began swirling through his body.

He passed gas.

"Ahh!"

Removing the needle, Dan sat back and enjoyed the rush of euphoria. His skin began to crawl, his heart picked up its rhythmic beat, and his dick grew rock hard in his shorts. Setting the needle to the side, he then moved everything and cleared a space on the desk. Turning, he reached beneath the mat on his bunk and withdrew the BUTT MAN magazine he rented. He opened it to a colored photo of a blonde chick enthusiastically sucking a long stiff dick.

"Oh yeah, sugar," he said pulling down his shorts. "You like suckin' white cock?"

The girl in the picture winked as her lips coaxed the cock.

"You bet'cha, baby," she replied.

Dan's imagination ran wild as he jacked off, turning page after page. His lust grew as the drug spread throughout his body.

In medical...

Unbeknownst to anyone walking the hallway, inside the Practitioner Assistant's office, where inmate screenings were conducted, Nurse Frost and Ted stole 15 minutes of their work day to partake in their adulterous affair. Sitting in a chair with his pants to his ankles, Ted concentrated while the nurse rode his dick. Her wet pussy juices covered his mid-section as she bounced to a heightened climax.

"I'm cummin'!" she growled in his ear.

Ted had his hands around her waist, balancing her on top of his rock hard pole. He watched as her hairless pussy lips slid up and down. Her pinkness erotic as her fingers massaged her clit. "Cum for me girl," he responded.

As she rode him, Ted watched as her titties bounced underneath her medical shirt. Her eyes were closed as if savoring the feeling his dick and her fingers gave. The fact that she was married always gave him caution but he knew that was the culture of C.O's; they fucked each other, period, point, blank. So as her body convulsed, he reached beneath her shirt and squeezed her nipples.

"Ahh... yes baby!" Nurse Frost came in short jolts of pure pleasure.

Ted had cum long before actually. The mouth of her pussy was so wet he shot a wad out from jump street. So as she enjoyed her fix, he just held her in his lap, slowly grinding his thighs.

"Nurse Frost? Hello, Nurse Frost," the call came from the other side of the door. The knob shook despite it being locked.

Snatched from her cloud, Nurse Frost recognized her coworker's voice. "Yes Tami, I'm uhm…" she jumped off Ted, their fluids running down her leg.

The young girl simply said, "Your husband's callin' you on the radio."

She looked and saw her radio on the counter. Its volume was cut all the way down. "Okay Tami, thank you."

Ted had already pulled up his pants and was buckling his belt. "Breathe. You look like your gonna shit a brick," he said humorously.

She ran her fingers through her blonde hair. She laughed and shook her head in disbelief. "I just need to get dressed. You got me so crazy!"

He watched her bare ass. Her figure was tighter than most chicks half her years.

Quickly, Nurse Frost dressed. But before she called to see what her nagging husband wanted, she slid into Ted's arms. "I love how you keep me on the edge."

Ted looked in her eyes and saw fire. She had fallen for him and he knew it. "Everybody needs a little spice in their life, baby."

"Is that right?" she replied with her lips perky.

Ted kissed her. "That's right."

The administration building held a wing strictly designated for SIS. Armed with the duty of securing, protecting, and monitoring all internal regulation of the prison, SIS was the FBI of the compound. As a whole, the officers selected as SIS officers were elite and had special interests in the field of corrections. So when Lt. Frost invited his 22 year old stepson, Adam, for a *trial run* at the job, he was trying to see where *elite* and *special* might apply.

Adam was 6'1" and very lanky. Wiry-thin, he was geeky with eyeglasses and all. Bone white with blonde hair like his mom; the kid stood at his step-pop's desk, fiddling with the remote control to his drone.

The phone rang. "Lieutenant Frost."

It was his wife.

"Oh, yes. I was just tryin' to let you know Adam started today. Yes, he's right here." He passed him the phone.

"Hey Ma," setting down his remote, Adam cradled the phone on his shoulder. "Okay… I gotcha. Meet'chu at the OM, at eleven. Gotcha, bye."

Lieutenant Frost stood from his desk. He had a lot of work to do but since Adam finally took up his offer, he decided to cancel all prior arrangements. This was important because he really wanted to help Adam find his path in life. "Alright, let's go."

Adam was back to meddling with his remote. "Where are we goin' now?"

"For a tour of the facility. Listen, you're gonna have to take this a little more seriously. Work needs to be done and put down that damn remote."

Although Adam looked distracted, his mind was actually clear and aware. Putting an end to his adjusting, he looked at his step-dad. "I understand that you're confused why I brought this," he said holding up the remote.

Frost tossed his hands up as if to say Adam was correct. He was confused.

"I agreed to check out the job for a few months, to see if my experiment would come in handy," Adam said.

"What experiment?" He knew Adam well. The kid's farfetched thinking had gotten him into trouble on too many occasions. "This isn't time for one of your hair brain experiments. This is prison. The real deal! With killers and child molesters and terrorists…."

"I know, I know. And security is the number one priority," he finished as if he'd heard it a million times.

"Exactly!"

Adam looked to clarify his intentions. "Okay, so look. This drone over here." He pointed to a stealth-like remote controlled miniature aircraft, which sat up against the far wall. "I think I can use it to monitor areas of the compound from several aerial locations. Something the conventional security system can't do."

Frost had not seen the drone sitting there. He remembered seeing it at their home and knew what it was. Adam and a lot of other kids were heavy into them. They were a part of every facet, including how law enforcement captured criminals on the street. Despite how crazy some of his stepson's ideas had been throughout his life, he had to admit the kid was on to something. "You can put a camera on that thing?"

"This is a Parrot BeBop drone equipped with an HD camera. It's light weight and will give me up to several hours of air time, up to four hundred feet in the air."

The lieutenant was listening closely.

Adam continued. "You told me to find something I love doin', and everybody knows I love electronics, video games and gadgets. Well, I was thinking if I could figure out a way to provide a system of drone security for this prison then maybe it would be the start of drones being used in all federal prisons."

A feeling of pride washed over Frost. He'd been in the boy's life ten years and this was the proudest he'd ever been. Pounding the desk, he put an arm around his stepson. "I must say, I'm really impressed. Adam, that sounds like a wonderful idea."

He smiled. "Mom thinks so too. She said you'd probably like it."

"Like it? I love it! And I do want you to pursue this. Whatever it takes. Let me know what you need. Matter of fact, I'm taking this to the warden and let him know what you're doing." He patted him on the back. "I think this little idea of yours might be great after all."

Adam smiled while tugging at the uncomfortableness of the uniform's tight shirt. Its starched edges made it feel like a brace around his neck.

In A-Unit...

Alexis was inside the office, chatting away on the phone with Erin. For the first four hours, the unit was relatively quiet and she hoped and prayed it stayed that way. Her friend on the other hand was working visitation. Both couldn't wait for their work day to be finally over.

"Hell naw girl," Erin said interrupting her.

"What... What's goin' on?"

"Hell naw," she repeated. "This fool sittin' here with his pants unbuckled, like can't nobody see him."

Alexis sat up straight in her chair. "Right there in front of everybody?" she asked surprised.

"Yep. And his girl try'nah play it off like she ain't got her hands on his stuff. They try'nah be slick with his shirt kinda covering."

"Who is it?"

"I don't know if you know that black guy, Wilson, in B-Unit," Erin explained. "Young thinks he's a pimp..."

"Dark skinned with french braids?"

"Yep."

"Girl fuck it, let 'em get they thang on," she laughed. Alexis felt they should at least be given conjugal visitations, then the prison wouldn't be so aggressive.

"Nope. The last thing I need is for people to start sayin' I'm lettin' them do it up in here. You know these dudes be tellin'."

Her friend was right. "Call SIS then."

Alexis hung up and turned to her computer. No sooner as she did, she saw a figure approaching her door. When she looked up her fears turned to reality when she saw some wanna be hip cat standing there, trying to be cute.

"Yes," she asked obviously annoyed.

The guy was around 30, mixed with something islander and built like an eggplant. "Sorry to bother you. But would you happen to have another commissary list?"

Hearing his request, she felt bad for stereotyping him. "Yeah, no problem," she said opening the drawer to her left and removing a few. "Here you go."

He stepped in and accepted them. His eyes locked onto hers. "Thanks, I gotta spend some of this long bread I'm working with," he said and winked.

Her guard went up. "Well gon' on and spend all that up outta here." Her voice hard and her finger pointing towards the door.

"Damn baby," he muttered on his way out.

"And my name ain't baby," she spat. That's when she noticed a small group of guys standing near the door.

They were laughing. "Man I told you she ain't feeling you," one said to the guy.

"Y'all fuckin' it up, standin' by the door," he replied. "Give me some space."

She couldn't believe her ears. *This ain't gonna get any better*, she told herself. And she knew that. There was no way she'd be able to keep them, or any man, from staring at all that ass she had. No way possible.

Just as she turned her attention back to the computer, she heard the jingle of keys. That's when she noticed her coworker, Leon, step in the doorway.

"Ms. Green," he said politely.

She recalled her demand to be referred to professionally. "Mr. Taylor," she said smiling.

"Call me Leon," he said stepping into the office and taking a seat in the chair opposite of the desk.

"Thanks for the company." Alexis leaned forward and placed her hands on the desktop. "So what brings you by Mr. Leon?"

Leon was always clean shaven, smelled good, and despite wearing the custom uniform, he always carried an aura of freshness. Smoothing out the wrinkles in his pant leg he said, "Well, I was just next door, working, and figured I'd come by the check on ya."

"Thank you. Don't I look like I got this? And if you're over here, who's watching your unit?"

His eyes roamed her fully perked breasts. "Naw baby girl, you got it. And the unit will watch itself. They're big boys over there. They got it."

The flirtatious innuendoes and hints of sexual energy vibrated from him strongly. Alexis just laughed inside at how his eyes jumped from her breasts, lips and hair. "So," she said leaning back in her chair, taking a more professional position. "You were here last year when the guy shot all those people from the tower?"

He nodded. "Yep. Crazy mutha'fucka. Ted used to drink with him sometimes. That war drove him insane."

"That's sad."

"Blew the warden's head clean off his body," he said. "I was there, you know? Brains all over my uniform."

"Really?" Her face was frozen in shock.

Leon held a straight face and then smiled. "Nah… I'm kiddin'. I was in Vegas partying. It was still fucked up tho'."

Alexi shook her head. "That ain't funny."

He laughed. "You should've seen your face when I said 'brains on my uniform'."

"Fuck you," she replied with a smile of her own.

"See, now that's more like it."

She looked at him and decided to keep it 100%. "Why you try'nah mack all this way?" As Alexis spoke, she looked him straight in the eyes, with a crooked smile on her face.

The question obviously caught him off guard. But Leon was too smooth to be tamed. "I mean… you're a fine sista. Plus being way out here from Houston, I figured you'd like a little company. Even if it is to show you around."

"Around where? Vegas?"

"If that's what you like." A gold watch and a few rings decorated Leon's left hand. He adjusted the ring on his pinky as he spoke.

Leaning forward and placing her elbows on the desk now, Alexis shook her head. "Look Mr. Taylor, I appreciate your compliments and yes it does get hella boring out here in the desert. But I can't be fuckin' nobody I work with. Plus yo' money ain't long enough to afford all this."

Hearing this, Leon immediately went into his back pocket and withdrew his wallet. He tossed it on the desk. "There's a MasterCard, American Express and thirty-five hundred in cash."

Alexis just looked at the leather wallet. Money green paperbacks were stacked and folded inside. But what he did next really impressed her.

"And you can have these too." Leon went into his Dickie pants side pocket and took out the keys to his 2019 Cadillac truck.

"Boy, you a fool," she said shaking her head.

On the yard, convicts sparsely scattered partaking the various activities they engaged in day to day. It was just past eleven, and already the sun was beginning to blaze. Dino stepped out on the activities move to get some fresh air and handle some business. He wanted to touch basis with a few people to see if some money could be made.

The Bloods were working out near the basketball courts, with Maniak and Donnie leading the group. Dino made his way over to pay his respects.

"Eight, nine, ten. Alright y'all, that's a wrap," Maniak announced to the small group of eight. He saw Dino approaching. "What's up big dog?" he asked, muscles bulging.

"Shit, that's you," Dino said pointing to his partner who was drenched in sweat. "What's up Ru?"

Donnie wiped his face with a towel. "Gettin' this money." His physique was stripped of all body fat as sweat covered his chest.

"That's right." Dino pulled a little closer to them. "So how's it lookin'?"

Maniak was the first to speak. "Everything's movin' real smooth. How 'bout on your end?"

"Ya boy Gordo sent that to my daughter. Plus, I got another five grand on the way. Half of that is for you."

Maniak nodded.

"How many ounces of kush we got out?" Dino asked Donnie.

"One and a half left. And I think my boy, Big Tex, try'nah get those. I'ma find out tonight."

"Okay, sounds good."

Dino looked and saw the Asians out playing cards on A-Yard. Lee and his boys seemed to be enjoying themselves. At that moment, the Asian looked up and their eyes met. They exchanged smiles and a quick head nod.

Everything's good, he thought to himself.

The fence that separated the yards ran near the courts so when they looked up and saw Bone approaching with a few Crips at his side, Dino, Maniak and Donnie stepped over to see how they were doing.

"What's up y'all?" Bone asked.

"Some ole shit," Maniak replied.

"Y'all peep the little meetin' goin on?

Dino looked towards the far end of the B-Yard and saw a small group of about four. Two were the new guys who stayed in his unit. "DC boys?"

Bone nodded. "Yep. I guess they try'nah get their shit together."

"Or maybe talkin' about that shit that went down in Coleman," Donnie added.

"The riot with the Florida boys," Bone asked.

"Yeah," Donnie continued. "I heard they had a few homeboys that ran."

On cue, Dino saw action. "Ohh, look…"

In the circle, Joe-Joe and his homeboys had another one of their DC homeboys, questioning him. Evidently, his name was associated as being one of the ones that left another one of their homeboys in the riot who ended up dying from multiple stab wounds.

Weezy was highly upset, grilling the guy aggressively. "Nigga, I saw you runnin'! You left T-Rock…"

Before the guy could respond, Weezy, Joe-Joe and Petey Moe were on his ass with closed fists, boots, and elbows.

"Wait, wait!" he yelled, unable to dodge the assault.

Weezy's closed fist combo caught the guy across the chin twice, dropping him to the ground. Like tag team wrestling, Petey Moe and Joe-Joe dropped hard boot bottoms on his head, neck, and chest area knocking him unconscious immediately.

"Punk bitch," Joe-Joe spat as he kicked the guy square in the mouth, sending blood and teeth flying.

Meanwhile in the gun tower...

The C.O. working, sat back under the electric fan flipping the pages to his American Curves magazine, eyeing the tanned beauties in the pictorial. He was so used to things being quiet that he didn't realize outside his window an inmate was being stomped into the desert's dust, only to be left there, bleeding and badly broken. Later the officer would be reprimanded. But at that moment, he was contemplating whether or not he should wait until he got off work to catch him a nut.

Ah, why not, he figured grabbing his hand lotion and some napkins out of his backpack.

Then the deuces went off, signaling an alarm and the commotion fucked his whole mood off.

"Dammit," he cursed when he jumped up and saw all the officers running.

2

"So what do you think?" Nurse Frost asked her son before forking salad into her mouth.

Adam shrugged. "Seems cool. If they let me use my drones then it would really be interesting."

The two of them sat in the Officer's Mess Hall enjoying lunch together. This was the first time they'd been coworkers and Nurse Frost was glad to see her only son finding his way in life. "I told Richard you'd be able to help around here. You're too smart to spend your time sitting around the house."

He took a sip of his cola. "I'm just glad I can be here so I can keep an eye on you."

"On me?"

"Yeah. The way you two argue at home, I can just imagine how bad it gets up here."

Nurse Frost shook her head. "We don't bring our personal life to work, Adam. And I don't need a chaperone either. Every marriage has its problems."

Adam shrugged his shoulders. "Well I say fuck him. I wish you would've left his ass a long time ago."

She looked shocked. Then with a stern glance towards the inmate working behind the counter, she turned her attention to her son and in a low voice said, "Watch your mouth around here. Our family business is our business. Do you understand?"

Humbly he nodded. "Yes, I do."

"Good," she said. "And when I'm good and ready I'll leave. But it will be on my own terms. Ya hear?"

"Yeah. I just feel like you deserve a lot more, mom. That's all."

Nurse Frost smiled at her son. He looked so much like his biological father. "We deserve more," she told him. "And soon

75

we'll have it. Until then, be a good son for me and do as he says."

Adam just sipped his cola and nodded his head.

Mid-day on the yard...

Bone and his homeboy, Tray, were walking the track when they saw Big Jake and a couple of his white homeboys. Tapping his Crip homie, Tray, looked to remind him of the promise he made in the kitchen.

"Aye Cuz... there go dat Wood right now," he said. "Ask him what's up wit' my bread."

Bone nodded. "Come on. We can get this settled now."

Big Jake and his boys were out on the yard enjoying the sun, playing a game of Pinochle when Bone and Tray interrupted.

"Hey, can we holla at you?" asked Bone.

Jake got up. "Yeah... what's up Bone?"

Both men knew each other from time they did at USP-Victorville before they tore it down. So Bone knew the big man was a stand up dude and man of his word.

"Big Jake look," he began. "Yo people..."

"Who?" Jake interrupted.

"Dan....."

The big dude shook his head already in disgust.

"...He owes my man right here."

"How much?"

Tray spoke up. "He's been owin' me eight hundred for two months now. And on Crip... I need that taken care of." As he explained, anger could be seen building up in him.

Big Jake looked to calm the situation. "Listen, Dan has been a problem and we were just figuring out how to handle him."

The white boys at the card table overheard the conversation and all nodded at Jakes comment.

"So," he continued. "Bone I need you to do me a favor. Get with your people. If Dan owes them, bring it to me."

Bone nodded. "Okay."

"And this ain't no free for all. I don't need everybody and their baby mama talkin' he owes them," Big Jake looked to clarify.

"Nah, I got'chu Jake."

"Good. As for you…"

"Tray… I'm from…"

Jake didn't care. "Get with me tomorrow. I'll send your money myself." The big man extended his hand to assure him.

Tray accepted and shook on it.

Back walking the track, Tray asked Bone. "So wha'chu think they gonna do to Dan?"

Bone gave a light chuckle. "If I know Jake, that big white boy is either gonna fuck him up himself. Or send someone. Neither choice will be good for Dan."

Inside the warden's office…

Maddox was meeting with his lieutenant to discuss tightening the security on the compound. Ever since the beat down incident on the yard, the warden was looking to install a few preemptive measures for outdoor activities.

"I'm thinking, we need more compound officers hovering," he said to Lieutenant Frost as they studied a blueprint of the compound's structure.

The lieutenant ran his finger where the sidewalk was highlighted. "I can see that working. Groups of two spread into several locations, like here, here and here," he said pointing. "They will circle A, B, and C yards on foot, following the outer walkways."

Maddox felt good about this. "Okay, we'll begin implementing this first thing tomorrow. We've got fifteen veteran officers transferring in from up north Atwater."

"Good. We need the experience."

The warden's office was plush, decorated with a cherry oak desk, bookshelf, and a small conference table. Thick burgundy carpet covered the floor wall to wall. When Maddox was appointed the position he added a little of his own touch of decorum. A few plaques, some floral arrangements, bobblehead sports memorabilia and such were delicately placed to give the office a home-felt vibe.

Taking a seat at his desk, the warden looked at his coworker and shook his head. "You know, this has turned out to be quite some job." He laughed thinking of the last year. "I never in a million years thought relocating out here in the desert would be this challenging."

Frost agreed. "Twenty years plus I've been working and this place has shown me more in it's infancy than any other place I've worked. Dempster was a tragedy. I just pray we never experience anything like that again."

Maddox nodded his head and said, "That's why I am placing a mandatory re-evaluation process for all of our new staff to be conducted by our psychology department here. Because there is no way in hell that shits gonna happen again."

Even though a year passed, the brutal shooting of Warden Dempster still haunted them all. The warden just prayed that the incident wasn't a precursor for things to come, like a bad omen.

In C-Unit...

Big Jake came from outside, marching in like a Roman Soldier. He was hot as fish grease and he knew it was time to deal with Biker Dan's bullshit once and for all. After he headed to his cell to grab something out his stash, he shot straight to Snake and Skull's cell to discuss the issue.

Snake was standing at the sink washing his hands when Jake opened the door. "Well look what the cat drug in!"

The cell smelled like alcohol, like usual. "We need to talk."

Skull was sitting at the desk. In front of him were several recycled bottles filled with white lightning. "What's up bro?" he asked taking a sip out of one.

Despite being frustrated, the big man broke down to them how the Crips came to him about Dan's debts. That made the fourth person that week, totaling an amount of over $3,000. By the time he was finished ranting, the bottle of liquor Skull was sipping on had been circulated amongst them until it was emptied.

"So what do you think we need to do?" Snake asked. His eyes red and watery from the strong drink.

"I say he needs to learn a lesson," Skull interjected. "That lil' bastard is trash that needs to be burned. Straight up! He can't control his habits so he needs a little tightening up."

Big Jake was still standing although the alcohol was burning deep in his gut. "Both of you really feel like that?"

Snake was the first to answer. "I sure do. Matter of fact, Eddie from Utah just told me Dan swindled him out of a couple hundred. Somethin' about a bad dope deal. He thinks Dan swopped the package with comet toilet cleanser. I told Eddie if it were me I'd kill his ass."

Jake heard Snake's case and made up his mind. Digging in his pocket, he removed the sandwich bag he took from his stash. "How would you two like to earn a couple grams a piece."

The sight of the pure crystal-meth glistening like shards of glass made both cellies' mouths water.

"Dan?" Snake asked.

Big Jake smiled in a devilish grin. "Exactly."

Skull popped the top on another bottle of white. "Well it looks like we're gonna have a party y'all."

Just like that a contract was put out to take out Biker Dan.

Meanwhile...

B-Unit was alive and buzzing with activity. With the temperatures too high for outdoor rec, the convicts in the unit preferred to stay inside under the cool air conditioning. The common floor area was sprinkled with chairs as some watched one of the eight 42" flat screens mounted from the ceiling, played cards or simply sat talking shit.

Dino was in the back with his unit team so when Mr. Carson let him into the unit from the side door, he headed straight to his cell so he could shower.

It had been a long day but things were going good. Ever since Dino got arrested and sentenced to 15 years, he spent his time in regret. The night he chose to help his "friend" do a robbery , instead of choosing his wife and

and daughter, was the biggest mistake of his life.

Now all of that was about to change. He was about to go home. With less than 24 months left, Dino went to his team review with his counselor and Mr. Carson and they told him they were going to recommend the full year halfway house.

Walking to the microwave area, Dino saw Slim with a few commissary items and preparing a meal. "What's up?"

Slim was chopping a beef log with a makeshift cutter. "Hookin' up a nacho bowl for the movie tonight. You just comin' back from work?"

"Nah, they just teamed me."

"What they say about the year?"

He smiled. "They told me they recommended it."

"You're gonna get it, watch," Slim said.

"Thanks. What's been up with you?" Dino remembered Slim told him about the chick getting at him on the website. Since then, Slim had been going to the store like crazy, and was even sporting fresh boots, sweats, and tennis shoes."

"Same o' shit," he said tossing the meat into a bowl before placing it in the microwave.

"You still got baby fuckin' wit'chu?"

Slim lit up and popped his collar. "Oh yeah, you know ya boy in there like swimwear."

Dino laughed.

"She's been holdin' the kid down," Slim continued. "And to keep it real…. She's the angel I've been prayin' for. Who would've thought a person with a life sentence would find love like I did."

"Love? Oh, it's like that?" Dino was smiling and genuinely happy for Slim.

"Yeah, man."

"Is she approved for visiting? I haven't noticed but has she been up here yet?"

"Not yet. But she's from Illinois and we figured it would be best to wait until after Christmas because it's gonna cost so much to come."

The microwave stopped and Slim removed the bowl. The fried smell of the beef log was strong in the air.

"Well that's good," Dino said. "Keep me updated."

"I will. When we get married you're gonna be my best man," Slim pronounced. "I swear, if you didn't write that letter for me I wouldn't even have her in my life. So thank you."

"No prob, Slim."

Dino headed up the stairs to Donnie's cell. He needed to get the numbers straight on how much tobacco and kush they had left. He knew there was a few ounces and cans worth in his stash spot in the staff's bathroom. Now he was coming to an end of his sentence and he wanted to generate as much money as he could.

On instinct, Donnie came out of his cell just as Dino was about to knock. "I was just about to come find you."

"What's wrong?" Dino asked.

His partner shrugged. "Nothin'. I was just comin' to holla. What's up?"

Dino told him he was recommended the year but they already expected that. As they spoke, they recognized the two new cats that came from DC stepped out of the cell next to Donnie's.

"Have you spoke to them yet?" Dino asked quietly.

Donnie shook his head. "You know me, homie. I gotta get to know you first."

Taking it upon himself, Dino looked to introduce himself to the new convicts. He felt they were black and race could mean a lot at the end of the day.

The two were standing against the rail. Dino approached the one with dreadlocks. "Hey, what's up y'all?" his demeanor hospitable.

"Wut up, slim?" the one standing next to dreadlocks responded, looking past his homeboy. His demeanor defensive.

"My name is Dino... I'm from Cali. I just wanted to know if y'all need anything."

The one with the dreads responded. "I'm Joe-Joe and this is my homie. We from DC. Good looking' out, but nah slim, we cool."

"Alright," Dino told them and stepped back over to his partner.

"What they say?"

"Nothin'." He told Donnie. "But I swear I know the one with the dreads. Said his name was Joe-Joe."

Meanwhile...

Joe-Joe and Petey Moe turned and headed down the steps. They'd been chilling up in Petey Moe's cell and were now going to Joe-Joe's. They hated being all the way out in California, but at least they got a chance to grab their own cells.

"I think I know o'boy," Joe-Joe said.

Holding his saggy pants up, Petey Moe took a look as Dino stepped into the cell next to his. "From where? Was he at Coleman?"

"I don't think so, nah," he said trying to remember. "But I've seen his face. I know it."

The Friday evening dusk settled in the sky like an old Western movie. It was like a big ball of flame wailing in the distance, on top of dry desert land. Uncommon was the light breeze that blanketed the area, almost relaxing the mood.

Inside the staff lounge, just under 40 employees and officers gathered in commemoration of the slain Warden Dempster. Maddox also wanted to celebrate a new beginning for USP/ADMAX Death Valley and its staff. This was a good opportunity for all of them to get to know each other. So with a buffet of food, cakes, pies, punch and champagne, everyone stayed late to partake in the fun and charades.

"So tell me what you think of the place so far?" Maddox asked Adam.

The young man stood with his mother and step-father while they both looked on, proudly.

"It's a good layout," he said. "Security could be a little tighter though."

The warden smiled. "I really liked your idea of drone-testing and want you to know I called Washington about it. They gave me permission to experiment and I'm putting you in charge…. I mean, if you want the job."

Adam looked at his mother who was beaming, then to the warden. "Why… why sure. I'd be honored."

"I'd need you to document it all in writing. Washington would want data if we were to continue this project. Could you handle that?"

"Definitely." Adam couldn't hold his excitement.

Him and the warden shook on it. Then he turned to his parents as the head of the facility went off to mingle.

"So how do you feel honey?" his mother asked.

"I'm just glad they're willing to give it a shot. Rich didn't think it would work," he said proudly.

Lieutenant Frost objected. "I never said it wouldn't work. Listen Adam, kid, I'm proud of you. Who knows, you may change how we view corrections with this."

He agreed. "This is the future. Trust me." As Adam spoke he saw the most beautiful woman he had ever laid eyes on. "Excuse me, I'll be right back."

They stood there a little confused at their son's behavior.

The woman was dressed in formal wear as they all were. No uniforms. She was standing next to another woman by the table with the drinks. Her body was stacked and toned. As soon as he came upon her, she turned.

"Ah… hello, may I ask your name?" he said nervously.

She smiled. "Alexis."

He stuck his hand out and she took it. "I'm Adam. Nice to meet you."

"Nice to meet you too."

Leon, Ted, and Hal were sitting at a table located near the back wall. Hal snuck in a bottle of Russian Vodka and they were taking shots out of the Kool-Aid cups.

"Fill'er up," Ted said to Hal who poured him another cup full. Ted slammed it down and looked at his watch. "I need to be on the road to Vegas right now."

"Damn I wish I could roll with you," came Leon. He sipped his kool-aid and vodka mix. "I gotta go to Loma Linda in the morning."

"Veterans?" Hal asked before downing his fourth cup.

"Yeah, my pops. I promised I'd go see him."

"I remember when my uncle was at that Veterans Hospital. They took damn good care of him."

Ted tipped another cup and said, "So how's that sweet tail comin', Leon? Don't we got some money on that?"

Hal lit up. "Damn right we do! We got one hundred bucks and you haven't hit that yet."

Now all three men were looking towards Alexis and her hot girlfriend, Erin.

"Ninety days hasn't passed yet," he said as he watched the new young white kid speak to her.

It appeared Alexis was doing her best to pay him little to no attention at all. As he spoke, she looked and saw Leon looking in her direction. When their eyes met, he smiled. She smiled back flirting also.

Leon turned to Hal and Ted. "And I almost forgot about the bet."

"Well I didn't," Ted said looking at his watch again.

Turning his attention back towards Alexis, Leon saw she had gotten rid of the kid and was now talking to her friend. When their eyes met again, she was drinking out of a straw almost provocatively. Since his advancements in her office, they'd been flirting pretty strong and this was taking the cake.

"Let me get another," he told Hal.

As Leon took a shot, he watched as Alexis headed towards the door. He wanted to get at her before he left anyway to see if maybe she wanted to ride out of town with him. It was worth a try. So he figured this would be a good time to see.

"Okay..." Ted told him. "You finally gonna make a move?"

He smiled. "You know me."

Leon came out of the doors and saw Alexis standing about 15 feet away at the end of the hall. She smiled. "Are you following me?"

Before he could answer, she turned up the hall. He then heard a door open and shut. Confused, he went to see what the hell the chick was up to.

The lights were off in the office when he opened the door. It was basically empty, an unused office space with only a desk sitting in middle of the room. Standing at the side of door when he entered, Leon came face to face with Alexis who confronted him.

"What do you want from me?" she asked with a straight face and a hand on her thick hip.

He tossed his hands up. "What you want me to say?"

"Say what's on yo' mind, little boy." Her comment was full of sass.

Leon liked it. "You know, you really talk a lot of shit. One of these days I'ma call you on it."

She laughed. "One of these days? Boy," she waved her hand around. "All you got is space and opportunity."

Tired of her games, Leon said to the hell with all the cat and mouse. Stepping into her, he reached to see her reaction. At first she hesitated but once his hands came in contact with her lower back he felt her body concede.

Leon pulled her to him, kissing her lips in a deep passion. She was hot and sucked on his bottom lip like a neck bone. He gripped her ass with both hands, pulling her body into his. She felt like hugging a mattress, soft at every angle. His dick grew rock steel solid as her hands slid up his sides.

She broke contact and looked at him. "Boy you just don't know, you playin' wit' fire," she said licking her lips. "But this time I ain't givin' you back yo' keys and wallet. Are you still interested?"

"Even more now," he said.

Alexis' eyes danced as she scanned the room. Then without hesitation, she turned to the small office window and closed the blinds and locked the door. Leon couldn't believe this girl was this bold.

Alexis backed up to the desk, pulling her pink iHEART RADIO t-shirt over her head, she continued on until she was buck naked before him. Then she sat on top of the desk, with her heels planted and legs spread, she exposed him to the fattest shaved pussy he'd ever seen.

"What are you waiting for?" she asked.

It took no time before he was naked from the waist down. His dick sprung out before him like a blind man's walking stick as he stepped in the dark towards her with his pants around his ankles.

Alexis gapped her legs and he closed the distance between them. Leon looked in her eyes the moment the head of his black meat stick came in contact with her hot opening. When their lips reconnected, he felt a wetness melt around him that gripped and massaged every pore in his dick. As he sunk deeper, her legs spread more, taking him steadily.

"Ooh," she moaned in his mouth. Alexis reached between them and found his balls. As he stroked his pole into her, she rolled them in her fingers, applying a slight bit of pressure.

The desk presented the perfect angle for Leon as he placed bullseye strokes into Alexis. With his hips, he thrust all ten inches into her body. Like a pro, she was taking it, gritting back from the pain he gave. Her pussy grew wetter and wetter despite its tightening around him. "Shit... girl, oooh," he grunted as she rubbed his nuts.

That's when she laid all the way back on the desk. With her legs sky high and spread in a V-position, Alexis shook her legs, causing her thickness to vibrate waves of pleasure on Leon. Seeing his dick wet from her juices and the thickness of her puckered pussy lips made him fuck her deep.

"Uhn! Uhhnn..." he pounded towards the feeling boiling up in his loins.

As Alexis' body shook, Leon couldn't resist the fiery feeling. Throwing her legs almost into a split, she flicked her clit in time to his thrusts until finally he pulled out and blasted a thick wad of cum into the air. It landed and spread all over Alexis' stomach area, as she continued to pop herself into a climax of her own.

Leon was woozy as his dick was still in a spasm. He stroked cum out of its head while sliding it up and down, across her wetness,

Leaning up on an elbow, Alexis dipped a finger in the cum he shot onto her body, then she stuck it in her mouth, sucking it like a miniature penis. "Umm... so are you satisfied?"

Without answering, Leon bent and removed his wallet from his pants. "Here," he said handing it to her. "Take it all. Every cent!"

Alexis just giggled. She knew she had him now.

3

The few white boys that rolled in on the bus informed Big Jake that there was indeed a major hauling of inmates underway. Word was close to twenty buses were in transit waiting to be shipped across the desert highway. People were being re-routed all over the U.S. to accommodate the new prisons need for population. Some were happy but most were upset that they had to leave their other location; only if they were from Southern California did they appreciate the change.

The only thing Jake was concerned about was establishing something for himself and the whites on the compound. He would not tolerate any child molesters, rats, or rapists in their car. If a white boy got off the bus, then Jake made sure they knew immediately that the only solution for any of these types were the knife. The few who came said they agreed with this policy.

Another thing that had been on his mind was Lee and how the bastard insisted on taxing him and his people, while reaching an olive branch of prosperity to the Blacks. Every day he saw him in the unit he wanted to press the man, or better yet run him off the yard. Lee had a hold on the gambling, tobacco, and drugs. The only thing the whites had was white lightning alcohol.

Truly an American travesty!

One of the reasons why Jake never put the bully game down on the Asian was because he wanted to see if he could figure out the man's game. How was he getting it in? Did he have an officer? Jake figured Lee had an officer because that was the only way he could stay so consistent with his product. If that was the case, and Lee had a police on his payroll, then all Jake needed to figure out was what officer and the pattern Lee used to have his shit dropped so each time he could put his extortion game down.

"TEN minute move!!! Open move!" came blaring over the P.A. system.

He was on his way to the shower when the activities move was called for night yard.

Jake had his towel, fresh under clothes and soap bag with him about to step into a stall. That's when he saw Snake and Skull making their way outdoors. Both were dressed in heavy coats and skullcaps. They looked up at him and gave him a head nod. It looked like they were about to make good on their assignment.

Outside...

The overhead compound lights shone bright, lighting an otherwise dark night. A few people hung out, enjoying the late night recreation. Not many USP's still ran open yard at this time of the evening so the convicts did their best to take advantage of this rare luxury.

Snake and Skull followed the walkway behind two other guys going into the unit next door to theirs. The plan was to sneak into the unit without being stopped or detected by the officer working that unit. Then to put extras on it, they both were hauling bottles of Grade-A white lightning. They felt confident in their mission because the place was so laid back, no one ever expected anything.

"The move is closed!"

When both men came to the unit's sliding door, they found the C.O. standing right there. He was an older Mexican man, probably with years of experience in the BOP. On this night, he slipped, letting them walk past him and into the unit.

Snake looked up towards the cell they were going to. "He's up there," he told Skull.

The light was on and Skull saw someone inside, peeking out the small window. "Yeah, Critter is looking down here now."

Making their way, the convicts headed towards the stairs. After reaching the cell, Snake opened the door and saw Biker Dan's cellie, Critter, standing there anxious. Biker Dan was sitting at the desk rolling up a cigarette.

"Hey there boys!" Critter said. His stringy brown hair a mess on top of his head.

Snake looked at him, and said, "Has this officer been doin' a lot of walkin'?

"No," came Dan. "Did y'all bring the bottles?"

"Right here," Skull said pulling out two.

Snake had one as well. Taking off his coat, he took a peek to see if the C.O. was going back to the office. He was, so everything was perfect.

Biker Dan noticed they brought the moonshine so he went in his locker and tossed them 20 books of stamps, equaling up to $120. Skull passed him the two bottles he purchased and with Critter, the four of them proceeded to pop bottles and smoke cigarettes.

The Sony radio played rock music that blasted through the prison constructed speaker box made of headphone speakers and an amp. *Another Brick in the Wall*, by Pink Floyd came on, setting the mood just right.

"Fuck, this shits good!" Biker Dan said, chugging a shot worth. He saw his cellie getting all cozy, slipping on his watch out duties. "Critter, get your ass on that door!"

Critter jumped from his squat on the toilet. "Man he ain't moved," he said looking straight out to the officer's station.

Snake and Skull were hogging a cigarette. They finished a whole bottle by themselves and the strong alcohol was working their limbs loose. Digging in his khaki pocket, Snake pulled out a small knot-tied plastic bag, with a tiny ball of meth in it.

Dan's eyes lit up. "Oh you brought candy?"

Snake popped the knot on the table next to the man. "Enough for a couple lines."

Critter looked at Biker Dan and knew he was going to be left out. Again.

"Well, line up three good ones," Dan said.

Using the hard plastic edge of his prison identification card Snake crushed the meth into three fine lines. Then making a small straw out of some loose paper, he hit the first line, snorting it clean.

His nose burned. "Whew!"

"Let me at it!" Biker Dan yelped.

Skull muscled in. "Hold your horses, champ." Taking the straw he bent to the desk and vacuumed the second line. Instantly his eyes watered.

By now Biker Dan was feeling like Critter, who was now looking like a puppy on Skid Row. "Let the master taste the rush."

Taking the quill, Biker Dan pulled the particles of meth off the table with so much force it blasted against the bridge of his inner nostrils like fire. The purity of the drug shocked him, as he tossed his head back to let it drain down the back of his throat. His eyes were closed yet they watered like crazy.

"My God!" he cried, wiping his eyes with the back of his sleeve.

The music played and his head spun in time to the strum of the lead guitarist's cords. *"....all in all, you're just another brick in the wall,"* the lead singer Roger Waters sang.

Biker Dan felt the drug eating through his system and he knew it was pure adrenaline. Slowly, he lowered his chin and opened his eyes. Three shadowy figures were blurred in his vision. He saw Critter still at the door with Snake and Skull towering over him.

"Yeah, that's the real deal," he stopped short at the sight of the eight inch ice pick in Snakes hand. "What the…"

Pop…Pop…Pop…Pop…Pop… Snake swung, sticking Dan in the neck and upper chest area. *Pop…Pop…Pop…*

With his legs flailing like fish fins, Biker Dan's body kicked against the bunk. Meanwhile, Snake stayed digging with his weapon. *Pop…Pop…Pop…Pop…*

"Ah…Ahh…I…help…"

Critter looked at the man who constantly disrespected him and smiled, then he turned his attention back to the door.

"You fuckin' piece of shit," Snake cursed pinning Dan's body while he butchered him.

The man was bleeding like a pig, leaking from the multiple stab wounds. Skull stood there looking into his eyes, froze in panic, as blood came gurgling out of Dan's mouth. His body began to convulse violently, causing him to kick hard into the locker.

Ba-Doom!

"Grab his legs," Snake ordered Skull.

"He heard it!" Critter announced looking scared from the door. "He's coming! The C.O.'s coming!"

Snake hopped off of Dan covered in blood. He looked at Skull. Nothing needed to be said. They were going out with a bang.

Next door...

Big Jake cut the water to the shower off. He dried his body, grabbed his belongings, and stepped out just as Lee was coming out his cell.

"The C.O.'s are running next door," Lee announced.

"Oh yeah?" Jake asked.

"Yeah, probably a false alarm."

He knew better. "Probably not. That's what this place need, more action," he said walking away. Then over his shoulder he added. "Maybe then motherfuckers will start acting right."

Lee stood there contemplating the meaning of the big man's comment.

Outside...

"Go! Go! Go!"

Lt. Frost sprinted across the compound as if he never had, not one but two knee surgeries. The last thing he thought was his overtime would involve responding to an assault. Over a dozen officers trailed behind him as they responded to the body alarm triggered by the officer working A-2's housing unit.

"Move! Move!"

Getting to the sliding door to the unit, all of the officers ran in behind the lieutenant. The inner door was unlocked and Officer Vasquez stood next to it, ushering them in.

"Upstairs," he said. "Two aggressors with weapons. One inmate is in critical condition."

"They're still in the cell?" Frost asked about the inmates.

Vasquez said, "Hell yeah... I wasn't getting involved."

Officers had already began running up the steps. Frost fell in the rear just as the door to the cell came flying open. An inmate covered in blood came charging out, waving a long slender knife.

"You fuckin' pigs!" he yelled as he rushed two officers.

With an arc, the inmate's arm swung, knife in hand. The officer closer made the mistake of dodging when he should have ducked and caught the unforgiving end of the sharp ice pick.

"Uggggh!" he cried, feeling its point dig deep in his shoulder blade.

The other officer behind him dove and tackled the inmate. As soon as he did, another inmate emerged from the cell, planting the front end of his black boots across the officer's face.

WHAMM!

Blood, teeth, and spit shot out of the officer's mouth, spinning him up against the tier's wall. He was out, cold.

The scene drew the attention of every convict in the unit as they all watched from their cells. Skull and Snake went renegade, fighting each officer until finally they were overpowered. With a combined force, the C.O.'s physically restrained the two men, battering them and breaking ribs in the process. It took almost five minutes to contain the situation before medical was able to tend to the assaulted inmate.

Lt. Frost stood next to the stairwell, his all white button down correction's shirt was splattered with blood. "Take them straight to the SHU," he said of the two combatants.

"Yes sir."

When he walked back to the cell, the cellmate of the assaulted stood up against the wall. "Take his ass too," he told another officer.

"But I didn't do nothin'," Critter cried. "They came in our cell and—"

Frost wouldn't hear it. "You can tell it to me another time. Tonight you're going to the hole."

The officer dragged him off.

The medical staff were inside the cell. A gurney was maneuvered in the small space to place the assaulted inmate on. Frost stood in the doorway looking at all the blood smeared on the walls and floor. It looked like a horror show. The inmate on the gurney looked even worse.

A nurse practitioner was tending to the gruesome looking man. He turned and looked up at the lieutenant. "He's not gonna make it," the young man said in a sad tone.

Frost shook his head. This was definitely not how he thought his OT was going to end up. He grabbed his radio. "All units… this is an institutional lockdown. Secure all inmates in their cells. I repeat… this is an institutional lockdown. Control, announce lockdown."

The PA system blared throughout the whole institution. "All inmates return to your housing units! This is an institutional lockdown!"

For the days that followed…

The administration was shaken by the murder. Case Managers, SIS, and other official staff conducted individual screening sessions with inmates in every housing unit. They wanted answers and Warden Maddox wanted them ASAP. So they pulled each and every person out of their cells, asking a slew of questions but to no avail.

As the convicts sat in their cells, for most it had been a long time since they were on a serious lockdown. Up to that point, no one had ever been stabbed, let alone killed. First, the beat down on B-Yard and now this brought well wishes for the things to come at USP-Death Valley. It was surely living up to its name.

The rookies got an opportunity during this time to experience working in a lockdown situation. From serving box lunches to showering inmates cell by cell, all of a sudden the job began to feel like work. It also brought them face to face with the fact that this was prison life, and they worked amongst the nation's most hardened criminals. Rookies like Alexis and Erin realized the one on the gurney could've easily been them.

As for the vets like Leon, Ted, Hal and the rest, this incident meant more overtime. One dead body would surely bring close to $70 per hour.

For a full week, the prison moved very slowly. Maddox planned to keep it all locked down way past the investigation the FBI was conducting on the murder. Once all of this blew over, he had another influx of inmates coming and he prayed that them arriving on a lockdown would send a strong message.

The blazing sun scorched in a cloudless sky once again. For miles, all the eyes could see was heat waves, parched earth, and from the right location, a 50 foot wall in the distance. The highway snaked through the California desert with slow traffic as usual. The only vehicles moving were 10 federal transportation buses, traveling back to back, with forty convicted criminals on each.

This was just day one of three to come. By the time the prison came off of lockdown, there would be close to 1,200 new inmates on the compound.

THE WALL

EPISODE 3
A VICIOUS TRIANGLE

1

The double-bladed propelled halo drone copter whizzed through the air like a dragonfly, barely making a sound. Moving up to 20 mph the 7x5 inch micro-craft sped along the prison walls only to stop and spin at the controller's command.

As Adam stood groundside, masterfully navigating the lone drone with his hand held controller Warden Maddox, his stepfather, and Captain McDaniels looked on. They all seemed impressed with his idea and now he was showing them the benefits drones could possibly make in the BOP.

"Okay Adam… bring her on in," Frost said after seeing enough.

Bringing the drone in, Adam landed it on the cemented area next to them. "So wha'chu think?"

The warden smiled. "I think you're ahead of your time kid. What do you think, Mac?"

The captain said, "Considering the fact that we just filled up a prison, this will help tremendously. I say we let this kid figure out exactly how we'd implement this into our security."

Buttoning his blue blazer, the warden looked at Adam in a serious manner. "So it's settled. I'll give you two weeks to draw up a plan for perimeter use that's outside the wall and an interior flight plan areas inside the wall. Give me specifics."

"Got'cha."

"And I mean specifics down to the tee," Maddox emphasized. "I want it to where someone can learn to operate that post for a three month period."

This moment was an accomplishment for Adam and he felt good. When the warden and captain both left, he took time with his stepfather to reflect on this opportunity.

"I can't believe they're letting me do this."

The L.T. looked at him and said, "It's really a great idea. I just hope nothing goes wrong."

"Why would you think that?" Adam looked at him and thought he saw a sly grin.

"Nothing... I'm just saying. Nobody wants to look like a fool, Adam. Me and your mother do work here."

Just when he thought someone had faith in him, he was wrong.

Fuck you, he thought as he turned to pick up his drone.

Leading the way to the door Lt. Frost said, "Now come on. You did a good job I'll treat you to some lunch."

In the warden's office...

The captain sat opposite of Maddox sipping a styrofoam cup of cold sparkling water. The heat outside was draining and now the inside air conditioning was giving back some of that energy. For the past three weeks, the two of them dealt with everything from the Internal Affairs and FBI's murder investigation to an over haul of new inmates.

In one wop, Captain McDaniels downed the cup. "Ahh!"

Maddox took a seat and leaned back, unbuttoning his jacket at the same time. "Drones? Can you believe it?"

The captain shook his head. "It's the signs of the times, my friend. In a moment, dudes like you and me will be extinct. They'll have iRobot running these camps."

"You're probably right," he said laughing.

"But honestly, I do think the kid got a good idea. An aerial view from a moving point will make us virtually one hundred percent secure, visually. Unless a person dug a tunnel, we'd catch all their movements on camera."

"Did you not see The Count of Monte Cristo," Maddox asked. "Or Shawshank Redemption."

The captain laughed. "That isn't happening in the desert, warden. Maybe on an island or back in the day. But not here, not in Death Valley."

Sliding up into a sitting position, Warden Maddox said, "With ambition and determination anything can be accomplished. Don't ever forget that. These criminals, some of them anyway, will do their best to get outside that wall. If we can prevent it then we will. But there is no one hundred percent way to ensure we will be successful."

"I understand, warden."

Maddox nodded. "I know you do."

The housing units were dead structures on the outside looking in and in Dino's it was as quiet as ever. The first thing he was concerned about was getting a cellmate. When he saw all the convicts they were bringing onto the yard, he couldn't believe it. With a cell facing the yard, Dino was able to see everyone they let out of R and D as they would all walk up the walkway to their assigned units. Never before had he seen anything like this since he'd been down. They brought small groups out with a co-escort almost every 45 minutes. One of the officers that worked his unit told him many inmates came in and they were being held in the SHU before being processed out. It was like herding cattle.

That was over a week ago and still he was a little skeptic about if he missed getting a cellie or not. He prayed he didn't so he could continue to enjoy his privacy.

Although the lockdown came unexpectedly, Dino was glad he had some commissary to eat. He hated the box lunches they served morning, noon, and night. Bread, meat, crackers, and Kool-Aid packs over and over again. On too many occasions he'd been caught without. Well, not this time, he had soup, peanut butter, oatmeal, fish, meat, chips, and snacks.

"Yo... Chi-Town!" someone called through the vents.

No response.

"Ayo, Chi-Town! O' boy who came off the bus!" the voice called again.

"Yeah! What's up? Who's this?"

"Ayo, you o' boy they call Rico?"

At that moment, Dino knew just by the way the conversation was going that this was an issue. Ever since the buses started arriving and putting people in his unit, cats had been calling out each other through the vents and doors.

The cat at the other end of the line was somewhere down the tier. He answered, "Yeah, my name is Rico. Who's this?"

"Is that Rico, who was at Beaumont?"

Momentary silence. "Yeah, I was at Beaumont. Who's this?"

"Bitch ass nigga you'll see when we come out!"

The guy Rico called out. "What?"

The other guy said nothing else.

Behind his cell door, Dino laughed. In his years down, he saw all kind of things occur. The federal prison system was too small for a person to think they could get away with anything. In the USP's it always came back around to haunt the person who messed up at another place.

The guy named Rico continued to call through the vent, getting a little irate at times. He even went to the extent of selling death to the guy inquiring about him. With things quiet, the little soap opera turned into entertainment for Dino, as he grabbed a change of boxers for a bird bath.

It was around 4 in the afternoon and Dino had just finished lotioning and getting dressed. He put on his sweatpants, tank top, and T-shirt to get comfortable. His radio was tuned into ESPN radio and Muslim oil hung mildly in the air. He was about to get a few packs of tuna out of his locker to make some sandwiches when he heard the doors being unlocked.

He shot to his cell door.

Yes, the officer was letting them out.

Dudes rushed to showers, microwaves and for cleaning supplies to clean their cells. When Dino's door was popped, he came out looking for Donnie. He knew something had to go down between the two cats beefin' in the vent. Their threats unmatched would never gain either of them respect.

Ms. Green was working their unit and Dino felt bad for her. If things got bloody between the two dudes, it could mess her up because she was a rookie. He thought about how Officer Taylor bragged that she had some good pussy and smiled. She did have a fat ass and she looked to be in good shape.

Yeah, this will be good for her, he thought as he saw his young partner coming out of his cell.

In the main corridor…

Leon and Ted were walking down the hallway discussing the latest. The bet that Leon wouldn't smash Alexis was won and paid immediately. Since then he became the Don Juan of the bunch, a master of seduction.

"I had the bitch crawling the walls!"

Ted shook his head and smiled. "How long y'all stay, all weekend?"

"Hell nah! Man, the Radisson is too expensive. We stayed one night," he said proudly. "She knew we had to get it in and get gone."

The door to medical unlatched and opened, Nurse Frost came out into the hallway dressed in her usual scrubs, holding some folders.

"Hey," Leon greeted her.

With a somber expression, she smiled. "Hi guys." It was obvious she wasn't in the best of moods.

"What's up girl," Ted said casually.

Her eyes were puffy as if she'd been crying. "Can I talk to you?"

Leon saw this as his cue to disappear. "Alright y'all, let me get up here to control. Ted…"

Ted nodded.

Once Leon was down the hall a bit, Ted looked at Nurse Frost, who was now cradling the folders in her arms. "What's wrong? What happened?"

She shook her head as her features began to crumple into a cry face. "That bastard hit me again last night," she said in a rough whisper. Her small voice full of anger.

"Hit you? The LT?"

Nurse Frost gave him a look that said he was being naive. "Don't let that discipline military shit fool you. That motherfucker is a no good drunk, who loves to play with more dildos than I do."

The image in his mind caused Ted to wince. For some reason, he saw the lieutenant dressed in his military uniform naked from the waist down, and bent over a La-Z-Boy. "Are you serious?"

Turning, she grabbed her keys and unlocked the doors to medical that she just exited. The small area was boxed in by another set of doors so their conversation was disclosed.

"I can't stand him, Ted," she revealed. "Although I've never cheated before you, I've always dreamed of running away with someone better."

He was confused. "Well, why have you stayed with him so long?"

"I wanted a fatherly figure for Adam. You know, discipline, military... all that bullshit," she said. "I just figured it would be good for my boy to have him in his life. But now, even he can't stand him."

"Does he know he hits you?"

"No, I haven't told him."

"He's never seen any bruises?"

She lifted up her shirt and at her lower back a red and purple bruise showed, fresh and swollen.

"Damn," he said.

"He makes sure they're not visible," she explained.

Ted could not believe what he was hearing.

Back in B-Unit...

Alexis finished opening the doors, letting the inmates in her unit off lockdown. This was her first lockdown and she had to admit the quiet was welcoming. Now she stood in her office doorway watching as they ran around like insects.

Dino met Donnie at the top of the stairwell.

"You hear them niggas woofin'?"

Dino was watching as one of the cats who had just arrived congregated with some other guys that just came. Their khaki pants, T-shirt and blue shoes distinguished them from everybody else. "Yeah, I think that's the dude trippin'?"

The guy pushing the issue was around his late 20's, 6'2" and at least 240 pounds. With a mean mug and swagger, he explained to the cats, obviously his homeboys, the details concerning the guy in question. There was about six of them in the circle.

Meanwhile, the guy in question, Rico, was off to the side explaining himself to two other cats who Dino felt wasn't buying what they were hearing.

"Nigga fuck that!" the dude tripping barked.

The guy who he said it shrugged too. "Fuck him then."

Dino and his partner watched with a few others in the unit.

The aggressor approached the guy Rico. "Nigga you hot!"

Being labeled as a snitch caused even more eyes to fall on him. "Man, I ain't that Rico," he said explaining. "I know who you're talkin' about tho'. Tell 'em D-Mack." He then looked at the guy next to him.

D-Mack stood there looking unsure. "Man, all I know is you was up there at the prison with us. I don't know…"

WHAMM!

The right cross whacked clean across his jaw sounding off a bone-crushing blow. Its impact knocked Rico's body, snapping his head backwards and smack into the concrete wall next to his cell door. He slid like a sack of potatoes with his head leaving a trail of blood from where it cracked open.

D-Mack and the other guy with him stepped off.

"Ah shit," Donnie said.

For a split second, the cats in the unit paused to look in the direction of the commotion. When they saw it had nothing to do with their people they continued on.

Alexis was on the phone in her office when she began to notice something strange in the unit. It seemed like the men kept looking at something.

"Did you hear me?" Erin asked.

"Huh? Yeah," she replied. "You said you've decided to go visit your grandparents instead."

"So what do you think? Do you think he'll be mad?"

"He'll get over it. Even if he does, it ain't nothin' a good blow job won't fix."

Erin laughed. "Yeah, you're right about that."

"Listen, let me call you back," she said. "I'ma walk the unit. I know you bored as hell."

"You're telling the truth. I'll never ask to work the tower again, especially outside the wall."

Alexis laughed and hung up.

"Excuse me..."

Looking up, she saw someone who looked like was a victim of a fatal car accident. The whole left side of his face was the shape of an grapefruit. "What the fuck happened to you?" she asked without really thinking.

He tossed his hands up. "I need to check into the hole."

Alexis never had anyone *check-in* before but by the looks of it, this guy needed to. His self-surrender to go to the SHU was obviously to protect his life.

She got on her radio and called the officers working the compound.

"B-Unit officer needs escort to the SHU... he's a victim..." Ted cut down his radio.

Nurse Frost stood with her arms crossed over her chest. Her eyes teared up. "I swear he'll never hit me again."

"And you shouldn't let him." Ted was upset himself. Never had he imagined the lieutenant to be abusive to his wife. Now the man looked totally different in his eyes. "What are you going to do?"

She shook her head. "I don't know."

"What do you wanna do?" he asked next.

"Honestly, I want to kill the bastard."

Her statement made Ted laugh.

"No, I'm serious," she said pointing a finger at him. "Between the life insurance and our assets... I'd be well off and finally free of his fucking ass!"

Ted stopped laughing. "Okay...okay...I see you're not joking."

Nurse Frost grew quiet. "Only if you knew how much I suffer," she said grasping his hand. The whole while she was conscious of anyone coming in and seeing them.

He smiled and rubbed her chin with his thumb. "That's what you have me for. To take away the pain." The Nurse did something to him and he knew it was sexual.

A smile spread across her face. "And that you do, lover boy. Actually, if it wasn't for you I would've probably killed him already."

Ted just laughed. "He'll get his soon enough."

Nurse Frost was no longer sad. Of course, before the two of them parted they devised a plan to meet for a quickie. She said she needed a stress reliever and he was willing to oblige her wishes.

Back in B-Unit...

Dino swore they were going back on lockdown. He just knew Ms. Green was going to panic and push the deuces when she saw the guy all battered and bruised. When she escorted him to the front door and the compound officers came to get him, Dino figured they just might make it.

Which they did.

The minor incident went by without anyone going down for it. The aggressor was now in line for a shower, his hand probably swollen. Their small group of homeboys were dispersed and Donnie was now on the phone. Dino decided to go to the computer to see if he had any emails.

The Corrlink Email System provided not only messages but also an option for a digital photo of the individual sending it. When Dino logged in, he saw that he had over 48 emails. Most were from family and a few friends. He clicked on one of the envelope icons and the smiling face of his 19 year old daughter lit up the screen.

H8 u'r on lockdown. Can't W8 'til u come home. B 2 C U when visits come back. Luv U.

Dino smiled. *I can't wait to come home either baby,* he thought to himself.

Upstairs in the unit...

Petey Moe and Joe-Joe stood on the railing, taking in the scenery. Both had been to numerous yards in the BOP's. This unit looked no different than the last. This was the first time the new arrivals were all out, and with them being new as well, they preferred watching things from a distance.

"Check out baby," Petey Moe said with a nod towards the officer.

Alexis strolled past cell doors looking in to see if everything was back to normal. The whole time she was well aware of the fact that she was drawing attention.

Joe-Joe looked in the direction his homeboy was referring to and saw nothing but ass and thighs. The C.O.'s confident swagger and good looks made him laugh. "They got these go-get it bitches, Moe!"

Petey agreed. "She's a rookie too, I can tell."

As she made her rounds, Alexis went up the stairs and proceeded down the range. Coming off the rail, Petey Moe gave her a lustful look. A look that made her stop.

"Uh... you got a problem?"

He chuckled. "Naa... dew you?"

His response made her square up her shoulders. "I'm not the one starin'."

Petey Moe shook his head. "Baby girl, you trippin'. Ain't nobody starin'."

"My name is Ms. Green," she corrected.

Joe-Joe looked to calm the situation. "Yeah, he got'chu, Ms. Green."

A second passed as she looked at both them. Then she turned to continue walking, peeking back at them only once. The self-assurance in her figure showed strongly as she switched her hips, bouncing her round backside in the tight correctional pants.

Joe-Joe just shook his head. *Damn that bitch is bad,* he thought.

2

It took another week after the inmates were let out of their cells to open up the recreation yards. So for the most part, movement had been limited to the housing units. On Monday morning, the yard was open unexpectedly and in a flash, it was full of people.

After an incident like the one that occurred, and such a long lockdown, it was common for the compound officers to be out in full force. For the three separate yards, six officers roamed amongst the small groups. As promised by Region and Washington, more officers were transferred to the institution to help establish it in the West Coast state. Warden Maddox and Lt. Frost made sure the new officers were debriefed on the vision and mission of the prison.

That morning was refreshing. With the sun bright and a few clouds drifting aimlessly in the sky, the inmates basked in the fresh air. While many milled around getting acquainted and reintroduced to men they hadn't seen in years, others played the various sports available and some simply worked out.

One group in particular gathered along the fence line was Joe-Joe and his homeboys from DC. Known to clique up with the inmates from Virginia and Maryland states, the collection of men in the group amounted to at least forty. Many of them were products of the incident that occurred in Coleman, so they were familiar with each other. Instead of wasting time shaking hands they discussed the immediate issue at hand.

Should they or should they not find and attack the guys out of Florida.

"Fuck them niggas," a cat named Butta from Virginia said, sharing his thoughts. "I say we merk every one of 'em."

"Yeah," came a dude name Jinx from DC. "They killed the homie T-Rock. I say we ride for shorty."

Joe-Joe knew this was a sensitive matter. He also knew they couldn't keep the beef alive if there was no threat. "Listen," he began. "Y'all niggas know me. I say fuck them niggas too. That shit comes and goes. We bodied four of them bitch niggas in my unit alone. They only got T-Rock. Yeah, he was my man too. That's four to one, not to mention them two niggas y'all got."

His comment was towards Jinx, who along with a few others from DC, butchered some Florida dudes caught sleeping in their cells. Jinx and his crew ran in and stabbed them multiple times leaving bloodied sheets, covers, and two dead men.

Joe-Joe continued. "I say we establish shit here... this new spot... because more homies is comin'. By that time we'll be able to transfer back home and the other homies shipped out here will fall right in."

Across the yard...

Dino and Maniak were standing against another portion of the fence line talking to Lee. Since their last shipment, things had been smooth. The lockdown put a small glitch in their operation but that's what they had stash spots for. They used the yard time to catch up on how much product was left and the next moves they planned to make.

"A lot of people came into my unit," Lee said.

"Mine too," came Maniak. "I was looking out the window and saw them taking a guy out of your unit, Dino."

He nodded. "Yeah, you know how it goes when one of them buses comes in."

"I knew there was going to be problems when they said so many were coming," Lee agreed.

Dino laughed. "The dude in my unit got messed up pretty quick too."

Maniak's attention was drawn to the DC boys. "Them niggas is politickin' over there."

Dino looked and saw the two cats, Joe-Joe and Petey Moe, from his unit. Joe-Joe had the others attention. "They're probably talkin' about that shit still."

Right on cue, Gator from Florida approached them. He gave Lee and Maniak a head nod. "What's up y'all? Hey Dino, Maniak ... Can I speak to both of you?"

Lee backed away. "Alright," he said to Dino and Maniak.

"We'll finish tomorrow," Dino said

Once they were alone Gator began to speak. "I know this is not your problem," he began with a look of extreme concern. "But that shit that went down with us and them DMV boys, at Coleman... me and my homeboys ain't try'nah bring that in y'all's backyard."

Everyone knew that Gator was a good guy. It was obvious that the Florida boys wanted no drama and were looking for help in the matter. There was no way Dino or Maniak were going to get themselves or their homeboys involved in the matter.

Dino was the first to speak. "What's the matter? Have they said something to y'all about it?"

Gator explained how in his unit, the DC boys pulled up on him. He let them know his position, and speaking for the rest of his homeboys. He did his best to assure them that issue died at Coleman. "But now I see them over there," he said nodding in that direction.

Maniak looked to shed some light on the matter. "I think if they were going to do something they would've done it already."

"That's real. So Gator, I'd relax if I was you," Dino agreed.

Gator exhaled a long breath. "Yeah, maybe you're right."

"Did y'all get some more homeboys?" Maniak asked next.

The old cat shook his head. "Not from Florida. We got a few cats from Georgia tho'."

Everyone knew Georgia and Florida cliqued up together.

Dino concluded the matter by saying, "I think Maniak is right. They're not tripping. Just make sure your homeboys do the same. Even when they come down the road, let 'em know that shits over with."

"Thanks y'all," the man said before walking off.

Once he was out of earshot, Maniak looked at Dino."That nigga is scared as e-mutha'fucka."

Dino laughed. "You ain't lyin'."

The meeting between the DC, Maryland, and Virginia guys was winding down. Several cats were relaying information they'd heard while in the SHU transit and other sources relating to the happenings all over the BOP. Some were commenting on their present cells and how they'd already began tearing down lockers and other metals in order to fashion knives.

Petey Moe was listening as Jinx spoke about some young chick who wrote him from Southeast DC, then all of a sudden his attention was grabbed. The first thing that he noticed was the tight form fitting pants hugging every curve and contour of the ass that passed. "Damn, who's slim wit' all that ass back there?"

Jinx stopped talking to see who his homeboy was referring to. A light skinned, long haired homosexual walked up the walkway, prancing all by himself. His khaki pants were styled like capri pants and his t-shirt was three sizes too small, hugged tight and knotted in the front. One arm swung side to side as he walked.

"Baby look like Alicia Keys," Petey Moe exclaimed.

Dudes nearby heard him and started laughing.

Jinx wasn't humored. "Nigga, I'm talkin' 'bout some ho's and you lookin' at that?"

Petey Moe waved him off. "Shit... them ho's can't take no dick from a nigga."

Joe-Joe shook his head. "Jinx, you know how that nigga is."

Jinx nodded. "Ol' freaky ass nigga."

While they clowned, Petey Moe's eyes stayed glued on the homosexual as he strolled the yard. He looked lost and Petey knew a lost sheep would always fall prey to the wolf. Deep down he could feel his insides howling.

Seeing his homeboy paying more attention to the yard pussy, Jinx turned to Joe-Joe. "So what happened to Champ?"

Joe-Joe explained how Champ got into it with the C.O.'s the day they arrived. "Slim was knockin' fire out they asses. They fucked him up tho' in the end."

"So he's in the SHU?"

"Yeah, I haven't figured out how to get at him either."

"Hopefully he'll send word," Jinx said finally. "In the meantime, we need to get shit poppin'. I got a few bitches out here."

Joe-Joe was a bonafide moneymaker. Knowing this to be a new spot meant a lot of loopholes in the system, especially with all the rookies. "You got some ho's willin' to bring that pack?"

He nodded. "Bitch betta do as I tell'er."

"Well, we need to figure something out," Joe-Joe said. "Somebody around here got somethin' movin'. Shit, we just want in."

High above the compound...

The faint whizzing sound was masked by the heightened noise of being out of the units and on the yard for the inmates. As they congregated, played, laughed and exercised not one of them spotted the octagon shaped drone hovering several feet above the four story units. Despite dipping into plain view and back over the top of the units' roof, the drone flew in and out, capturing video of all movement yard side.

As Adam sat in the cubical area assigned to his special duties, he monitored the drones flight, video, and audio. With an earpiece, he was able to hear as well as see. So with this capability he controlled the drone by remote, thrilled at the barriers he was breaking in prison's security.

"There you go baby," he said steering the knobs with the precision of an aircraft pilot.

The aerial view from the craft shone multiple groups standing about engaged in discussions. Adam knew at any moment a full-blown riot could kick off, causing harm to so many. His duty was to recognize threats such as knives being passed, drugs being sold, or other violations of federal rules. As for now all seemed calm.

Back at ground level...

Dino was cutting across the yard looking at his watch. He prayed they'd call an inbound move so he could go in and call his daughter. As he made it past the handball courts, he saw his Paisa partner, Gordo, waving at him by the fence so he headed over.

"Such a hard man to catch," Gordo said smiling.

"Who me? Naw, I'm always gonna be in the same place," he said jokingly. "I wish I could disappear. What's up?" Since selling the Mexican the cell phone, Dino hadn't really seen him.

"Everything has been great," the man said. "I've been able to contact family I haven't spoken to in years."

Dino had heard from Gordo's own mouth how difficult it was to speak to his family, who were still tied to the Cartel. So he knew the cellphone was a blessing for him. "I'm glad to hear that."

"But enough of that," Gordo said with a dismissive wave. "I was looking for you to make a proposition."

"Proposition? Like what?"

Lowering his voice, the Mexican drew closer to the fence. "How would you like to make one hundred thousand dollars?"

At first Dino thought maybe he'd heard him wrong. "Shit, who do I gotta kill?"

Gordo laughed. "No one."

"No one? Well, nobody pays that kind of loot unless they want somebody dead or held for ransom."

The Mexican snapped his fingers. "Ransom! I like that. I'll pay you one hundred-grand for my ransom."

Now Dino was really confused. "Ransom you, like how?"

"My freedom," he explained. "The money will be for you to ransom my freedom out of this prison."

"I still don't understand. Exactly how am I to help you get out of here?"

Gordo smiled. "The same way you get everything else into this place. Only in reverse."

Dino looked at how serious the man was and thought Gordo must've lost his mind. The $100,000 dollars had him imagining sticking the man in an oatmeal bag and Maniak tossing him onto the back of the delivery truck on the kitchen's back dock.

He laughed. "Gordo, you're a loco son of a bitch."

Gordo shook his head. "Yes, I know my friend."

The evening came and not a single incident occurred. This was not uncommon after keeping the convicts on lockdown for so long. Unless it was a major incident between the cars, for the most part, the issue would die down and everything would go back to normal.

Since losing his two comrades, Big Jake reassessed his position on the prison and how he saw the whites fitting in. The lockdown gave him some time to think. Then once they came off and he saw how many other peckerwoods landed on the compound, he knew the importance of them being established. USP politics would not allow a weak group to be on the yard, especially the whites.

So with more brothers, Big Jake hit the yard and introduced himself. A mixture of white boys came; some Aryans, Independents, a couple from Texas and a few Dirty Whiteboys. Several issues amongst them were discussed with Jake aiding in a temporary trace between the DWB's and Aryans. As a whole, it was barely one hundred of them. Their best bet was to coexist in the new place.

Big Jake went back in the unit. All of the excitement of being off lockdown had him tired and ready to relax. He thought he saw a good prison movie coming on FX so after his shower he grabbed his chair and headphones, and made his way towards the television.

The whites sat in a section directly in the middle of the unit with the Mexicans and blacks at either side. Their unit got nine more white boys and all of them were seated around the table.

"Hey there brother," a stocky bald-headed white guy said to him. The man was no older than 35 years old.

Jake knew he was an Aryan. "Hey."

THE WALL

The guy introduced himself as Dingo. Sitting next to him was a few other guys from Kansas and the Midwest. Another older white guy named Harley, sat against the wall. He was a part of a motorcycle gang called the One Percenters. He told Jake he was a high ranking member.

Scooting his chair up to the table, several of the whites moved to give him some room. Big Jake was just about to take a seat when he saw Lee peek his little head out his cell door.

"Aye Jake," the man called, waving him over.

What the fuck do you want, he thought as he headed in that direction.

When Big Jake got into the cell, Lee was already seated. "Close the door for a minute."

Closing the cell door Jake said, "What can I help you with?"

"Your people. If any of them are interested in buying some crystal meth let me know and I'll work you a deal."

Big Jake looked at this little man and it took all his might not to rush him, and crack his skull in half. "Listen, I've been trying to get you to deal with me on fair terms. You give these fuckin' monkeys prices lower than you give me. So until you start playing ball right, don't expect one white boy to spend a dime with you or that fuckin' ticket you run."

Lee didn't see all this coming. His face was frozen.

"If I catch a single Peckerwood doin' business with you and your people, I'll stab 'em myself," Jake concluded. Seeing the Asian had nothing to say, he opened the door and went out to catch his movie.

3

It was late and the institution was on lockdown for the night. With all of the inmates in their cells, the staff on duty relaxed, enjoying the peace and quiet. The increase in population made the first week off lockdown hectic, with officers rotating shifts to new units to multiple emergencies. A few incidents occurred where fights broke out, leaving several wounded and beaten.

Nurse Frost was working late. She relished in the overtime hours because it looked so good on her check. Medical was quiet with only her and another female working in the dentist office. So alone she worked in the nurse's office, sorting through some files on her desk.

That's when she heard the door open. It was her husband.

"Well hello," he said.

His presence made her night feel darker than it originally was. "Hey."

The LT folded his arms across his chest and leaned up against the door frame. "I just wanted to come check on you."

"I'm fine," she replied not taking her eyes off the files she was sorting.

Her tone made it clear that she was upset. "Can we talk about last night?"

Nurse Frost stopped and looked up finally. "Talk about what Richard?"

"Listen, I just wanted to say I'm sorry, okay? Is that too much?"

Throughout their relationship, the last five years had been complete shit for her because the beatings began. Overall, she never really loved him or his fetish ways. Originally, she was seeking security and a relationship with him seemed to provide that so she married him.

"Well I'm not looking for an apology," she said. "I'm lookin' for you to be a man, which we both know just isn't in you." Her little remark caused him to stand up straight.

"I tried to be nice about it but since you insist on being a bitch, I'll leave." He turned to open the door.

"You're more of a bitch than I'll ever be," she spat.

With a look of a raging bull, he stopped and advanced in her direction. His finger was pointed stiffly. "If you think I'll continue to let you disrespect me, you're losing it. Now I'll tell you once and for all, our issues at home will not be brought up here to our jobs. I won't let a slut ruin my reputation as an officer. Even if she's my wife."

"A slut?!" Her face shown pure disgust.

Lieutenant Frost opened the door. "You heard me right. See you at home." Then he slammed it shut, leaving her to wonder what he meant by his comment.

The following morning, a chill blanketed the prison that called for thermal sleeved shirts or a sweater. Nurse Frost wasn't able to sleep all night, other than the few hours she managed to catch just before her alarm went off. After the argument with her husband, she expected them to go home and get into another fight. Instead, she found her place empty.

He probably settled on a motel in Blythe, she figured. *Maybe with some long dick lover.* The thought made her laugh and jealous all at the same time. Nevertheless, it caused her to stay up wondering exactly what she was going to do about him.

Sitting in her car, she contemplated her options. A divorce was too easy for him. Plus, he'd battle her in court for the house and other assets. She knew it was coming to this one day but she never thought it would be so soon.

When she saw Ted arrive to work, she flashed her headlights at him. A surprised look came from him as he parked before getting out and making his way over.

She rolled down her window. "Well, hello there."

"Good morning to you also," he said. "Why are you sitting out here in the parking lot?"

"Hoping to catch you," she said. "Got a sec'?"

He looked at his watch. "Yeah, I still got forty-five minutes before I gotta clock in."

Ted rounded the car and got inside. The warm air blowing through the vents was welcoming. Settling in, he turned and saw something was bothering her. She noticed he recognized it so she went ahead and expressed what was on her mind.

"I think he knows."

At first, Ted seemed a little confused. Then it hit him. "Your husband?"

"Yeah, I think he knows we've been foolin' around."

"What makes you think that?"

She shook her head and said, "Somethin' he said last night. He came and found me in medical, called me a slut and said I wasn't going to make him look bad on the job."

Ted listened, trying to assess the information she was giving him.

"I just wanted you to know," she said in conclusion. "Just in case he approaches you."

"Approaches me?" he said with a chuckle. "His best bet will be to…"

"Oh shit, here he comes!"

Her words came just as Ted recognized the lieutenant coming towards the car. The look on his face said he meant business. Pulling on the door latch, Lieutenant Frost snatched it wide open.

"You bastard!" he growled grabbing Ted by the collar and physically removing him from the car.

Nurse Frost screamed. "Richard! Richard, stop!"

The LT was in a zone. Ted swung his arms up, breaking the hold on him.

"Get your fuckin' hands off me!"

Hand to hand military combat training took over, sending the lieutenant into Jet-Li mode. Ted's aggressive move was countered by two quick plain jabs Frost threw before Ted could blink. One jab hit Ted on the bridge of his nose and the other in his gut.

"Richard!"

117

Ted immediately lost all the air in his lungs and doubled over. Both his hands held a now bloody nose. "Agggghh!"

The LT shot a crosskick low into the back of Ted's knee, buckling him next to the car. Then he spent a thick soled Hi-Tek boot slap across the man's face.

Wham!

He knocked Ted's head into the car door, knocking him out at the same time.

"Oh my gosh!" Nurse Frost yelled. "You asshole!"

With the commotion being right outside the administration building, and it being shift change, the small confrontation didn't miss drawing a small crowd.

Lieutenant Frost stood over Ted and spat on him. "You'll never be me!" Then he walked off.

Nurse Frost ran to Ted's aide. Now with his eyes wide open, he looked like a train hit him head on.

Over in B-Unit...

Every morning Joe-Joe woke up and went into the workout room where he would do five hundred burpies. He prided himself on being in great shape. With no body fat and an 8-pack washboard stomach, he couldn't wait to hit Myrtle Beach. The idea of Spring Break snow bunnies was enough to go even harder.

He was in the room sweating good. Stripped down to his shorts, he went up and down in the routine, in front of the rec room's plexiglass window, he exercised. He was down to his last fifty when he saw Ms. Green coming out the office. Joe-Joe wasn't a fool. He was noticing she was doing that lately. He smiled, continuing his routine.

As he counted down, he kept his eyes on the female officer. She was making her rounds downstairs. Once she finished the bottom, she climbed the steps on the side the rec room was on. They locked eyes and he saw her look at his body.

He smiled, dropped, and hopped back up, his member swinging freely in his shorts.

Making it to the top of the steps, Ms. Green opened the door. "Excuse me…"

Joe-Joe stopped. "Yeah, what's up?"

"Can you put a shirt on? Ain't nobody try'nah see you like that."

One thing he knew was that female officers used all sorts of tactics for defense mechanisms. He laughed. "Are you serious?"

In an all too serious face, she said, "Yes, I'm dead serious."

Joe-Joe stepped towards her. His towel was now in his hands as he wiped his face and chest. "You've been workin' this unit almost a whole quarter. So you know I do this every day, why you trippin' now, huh?"

She smacked her teeth. "I'll trip when I get ready."

"Why you stay frontin' with all that attitude? That shit ain't cute, Ma'?"

Ms. Green stepped in and let the door close. "Who you think you're talking to? I ain't one of yo' fuck bitches, nigga! So watch how you address me." Her hand was on her curvaceous hip.

"Did you just call me a nigga?" Joe-Joe started really laughing. "Yo, baby girl, you are crazy as fuck!" Then he started clowning. "I knew you were ghetto but not ratchet."

"Fuck you!" she spat. "And go put a shirt on."

Joe-Joe saw her eyes on his chest as she turned to walk out the door. "Wit' all that ass," he said loud enough for her to hear.

She ignored him.

As he gathered all his stuff, Joe-Joe found himself humored. He knew when he ran across a female officer willing to break a few rules. He was a master of the game. What he just witnessed with Ms. Green gave him a new outlook on being at the California facility. He knew if he stayed around any woman long enough she would break under his will. That's what he was known for.

Breaking a bitch down.

While B-Unit was stirring with inmates making coffee and waiting for breakfast to be called...

Big Jake sat sipping a hot cup of Folgers. Ever since he checked the hell out of Asian Lee, he was keeping himself out of all the bullshit. There were new Whiteboys in the unit and he wanted to make sure they knew their place and stayed in line.

"Good morning," Dingo pulled his chair up and spoke.

"Good mornin'," he replied.

The older cat named Harley had moved off of the wall where he came into the unit sitting. Now he was up and close by Big Jake. "There's the two of ya, there," he said sitting his chair down.

Jake just nodded. "Hey." Since arriving, he kept his eye on the biker. There was something to him he couldn't put his finger on. The way the man bragged, Jake felt he was trying to be something he wasn't.

"So wha'cha guys watchin'?" Harley asked taking a seat.

"Spike TV," Big Jake said.

Dingo added, "Gangland. They're showin' motorcycle gangs. Maybe they'll show the One Percenters."

Right at that moment, the show came back on. Big Jake blocked the unit out, listening as the narrator of the show documented each scene.

"....So many agents trained to infiltrate the chapters. One bike club targeted by the FBI was known nationwide for its suspected involvement in the selling of narcotics. They go by.... The One Percenters."

"Ah shit Harley," Dingo said socking the man on the shoulder.

"Yeah, I see 'em. Those are my brothers."

The narrator continued. A man spoke on the screen. They only showed a silhouette of him and his voice was computerized.

"I went undercover when an informant of ours gave us the tip that thousands of pounds of crystal meth was being shipped from Toronto to Ohio. I knew the information was

reliable because the informant had just received a thirty year sentence and was trying to get his time reduced."

"Fuckin' rat!" Dingo spat. "Harley when did this…"

The man was gone.

Big Jake continued to listen as the narrator explained.

"The informant was a two bit hustler out of Colorado named Earl "Harley" Cunningham. When Earl—"

When Jake saw Harley's picture pop on the scene, he pulled his earbuds out and got up.

Dingo was pointing at the picture, along with the other Whiteboys. A few others walking by had now stopped and was watching the show.

Big Jake looked around and saw Harley at the office door talking to the C.O. With long strides, he made his way over there.

"Yeah man, I gotta go… man get up," Harley was saying. "Call compound man… I can't stay here."

Unbeknownst to him, the officer was Ted. He was suffering from the bruises he got getting his ass kicked in the parking lot and he didn't give two shits about what Harley was talking about. "Man, get the hell out of my office. Whatever you've done…"

Wham!

Big Jake slapped the shit out of Harley, knocking the man on his ass. "You piece of shit!"

Ted did not move.

Harley coiled on the floor. "Please man, they're lyin'! I'm serious! It's all a lie."

"You get the fuck off this yard or I'll kill you myself!" Big Jake's voice roared.

"Okay. Alright, I'll get his ass out of here," Ted said. He looked at Jake. "Big guy, I don't hit the deuces and I don't care for rats. So you might as well take it back to your cell before the compound officers come to get him."

For a moment, Big Jake paused. He was so heated that he almost missed the fact that the officer could've sent him to the SHU. He was familiar with him because he worked their unit.

But this pass showed Jake this officer respected the convict code. "Alright," he told the officer before heading to his cell.

The compound officers came and got Harley with the whole unit watching. Ted told him he should be happy he didn't get killed. Once the situation was over, he headed to Big Jake's cell, finding the man looking out his window.

"Hey man, thanks for not sending me to the hole," Jake said. "Dude was a piece of shit."

Ted nodded. "Don't trip."

"Well, anything I can do to repay it, anybody get out of line, let me know."

With his eyes swelling more and more, Ted nodded. "You know what? I just might take you up on that."

Jake didn't know how to respond. He watched as the officer closed his door and then turned back to the view of the compound from his window.

EPISODE 4
WALKIN' THE WALK

1

The SHU comprised of three, two-tiered ranges made up of twenty five cells a range. Two inmates per cell. The officers never had to deal with many convicts. No one really got in much trouble. Now that the buses were rolling in, the SHU was beginning to find more and more occupants.

A couple months had passed since they killed Biker Dan and now Skull and Snake awaited their fate. As cellies in the SHU, the two had turned the small cell into their new home. With a shower, sink, and toilet they managed to get all their property and some food. They also had radios so that gave them some form of entertainment.

Snake had just finished doing some pushups. All the meth and cigarettes he was smoking left him in bad shape. "Aye, tell me about that little chick you met in Tulsa," he said taking a seat on the metal toilet.

Skull was lying back in the bottom bunk reading an old book by Steven King. He knew his partner loved hearing about the adventures he experienced on the run from the feds. Sitting up, he sat the book aside. "Patty," he began. "From Muskogee, Oklahoma. Only eighteen years old. Said she wanted to be my Bonnie."

Snake's facial expressions showed he was all ears, and interested. "Pussy tight?"

"Tighter than cat's ass." Skull started laughing. "She was a rebellious little bitch. Ran away from an abusive home. When I saw her at that gas station that night in Tulsa, I knew she was gonna be hell."

Skull explained how we were traveling from Kansas in a stolen car and stopped through Tulsa to steal another. When he pulled into the Quick Trip gas station, he saw a car sitting idle right in front of a pump.

"I parked next to it and when I jumped in it, this blonde teenie bopper jumps into the passenger side."

"What she say?"

"She said she was goin' where ever I was goin'," he told him. "I didn't say shit, but dropped the car in drive. That night we ended up in a Motel 6 in Muldrow. I sucked that little puss and shoved so much dick in her that night that I drove her mad." Skull said they woke up the next morning to the sound of the motel clerk knocking on the door. After getting put out, he said Patty gave him an idea that set them on a two week run, breaking the law. She proposed they rob a bank. "Bad little bitch," Snake said. "Could she suck a dick?"

Skull smiled. "At first she couldn't."

Both men began laughing.

Commotion outside their cell came. It was somebody yelling behind a door.

"Aye C.O.! Hey pussy-ass police!"

Snake got up from the toilet and looked out the window. "It's that loud ass black fucker again."

Across the hall, on the opposite side of the tier, was a black dude who had been back there about as long as them. "What the fuck is he cryin' about now?"

On cue the man banged on the door. *Boom! Boom! Boom!* "C.O.!" *Boom! Boom!* "Where the fuck is the…" *Boom! Boom!*

Each range had a barred gate that allow access. Keys jingled as an officer unlocked the gate and made his way down to see what all the commotion was.

"This asshole just called the police," Snake said in disbelief.

The officer was a short, fat Hispanic man in his late 40's.

"Why are you beatin' on my door?"

On the other side of the tier…

Champ was pissed the fuck off. He'd gotten some mail that was backdated, informing him that his mother had passed away. "I need to see the Chaplin about a phone call."

The C.O. said, "Is that what you're making all this noise about? You use the phone like everybody else, once a month."

Boom!

He struck the door with so much force the officer jumped. It's almost like the door threatened to burst off of the concrete which held it. "Man, fuck that! I need to see the Chaplin, it's an emergency."

"Wha-What kind of emergency?"

"Family… it's personal!"

Seeing he was really upset, the officer said, "Alright, but calm down. Let me go call 'em."

Now, huffing and puffing like a raging bull, Champ tried to calm his nerves. Once the officer left from in front of his door, he saw the white boy looking over at him. "What the fuck you starin' at redneck?" he barked.

"A loud ass rap-monkey," came the response.

Champs face twisted in disgust. "Bitch, I'll kill you."

Snake laughed. "Well, we know you'll kill the shit out of a cell door."

His breathing picked up. Balling his fists, it was going to be some time before Champ calmed back down.

On the yard…

Things were shifting on the compound. With more inmates outside, recreation was in full swing. Adapting to the new conditions found the convicts quickly adjusting into their new home. Cats went from simply grouping to mingling amongst each other. Different cars and gangs were sharing activities, as many knew each other from different spots. The hustlers were expanding, tobacco, weed and meth were the drugs of choice.

Joe-Joe was sitting outside, watching as his homeboy, Jinx, opened up his poker table. This was an old venture Jinx had going, one he did at every spot he went to. The rest of their homeboys stood around the table or against the fence joking on each other and talking shit.

Petey Moe walked over. "Man, it's hot as a mutha'fucka! This Cali shit is overrated."

Joe-Joe agreed. "The sun don' went down, but not the heat."

"La Soda...La Soda... La Soda..." a small Paisa man said in his best english. He was walking by, carrying a large plastic bag full of ice and sodas.

"Hey... Migo'," Petey-Moe called out.

The Mexican turned quickly towards them.

"Yeah, give us two."

"Two for five stampas."

Joe-Joe watched as his homeboy pulled out a stack of stamps to pay the man.

"Thank you," the Mexican told them both before leaving.

"What did you do, buy some stamps?"

Petey-Moe handed him a soda. "Nah, the Crip at the table owed two hundred. So he gave Jinx a few caps of weed. He gave it to me so I've been sellin' that shit."

Joe-Joe turned and saw the guy taking a seat at the table. "Was it that exotic?"

"Yeah, that neon haze bubblegum kush. It was loud as fuck. You wanna stick?"

He shook his head. "Nah. Tell Jinx to see if he's try'nah sell us some."

"I will." Petey-Moe's attention got distracted when he saw his new obsession. "Oooh, I'll be right back."

The light skinned, long haired homosexual was walking up the walkway, towards an unoccupied bench. Joe-Joe watched as his homeboy two stepped over to him, making conversation.

"Man that nigga ain't changed since I met him ten years ago in Hazelton," Butta said walking up.

Although he didn't agree with his homeboys preference, Joe-Joe never judged the man. He knew Petey-Moe was more reliable than most of them and would push a knife faster than he'd push a stroller. "Have you figured out what you try'nah do out here?"

"Well," Butta began. "I got a line on some sugar and was thinking about makin' some fire ass wine."

"Shit, they say the Whiteboys cookin' shine at this bitch."

"I was thinkin' about that too."

"Good, 'cuz we gotta get some money." Joe-Joe watched Petey-Moe, who had the punk laughing. The two of them had spoken on a couple other occasions. He knew it wouldn't be long before his homeboy moved the dude in. "What about the knives?"

"All of us in B-One workin' now. We should get at least fifteen joints out of that metal."

They had come up on some scrap metal strips, a quarter-inch thick. When the place began to fill up, some of them were moved into units that had never been occupied. The strips were left behind by construction crews as trash. For prisoners like them, this was equivalent to dropping a case of AK-47 in the middle of the ghetto.

There was bound to be killing.

Joe-Joe seemed pleased. "As soon as you get the first one made, shoot it to me. I feel naked around this bitch."

"I got'chu," Butta promised.

"And make sure it's razor sharp."

Exiting B-Unit...

Dino and Slim were on their way to a visit. Dino's daughter came like she promised and Slim's internet girlfriend finally made it to see him. Since all this occurred, Dino watched his partner go from hopeless to happy and it was good to see Slim energetic.

"She came all the way from Illinois," he was saying. His Armani scented Muslim oil was strong.

Dino was listening but looking around for Gordo. Since the Mexicans inquiry about paying for help to escape, Dino had really been thinking about it. Plus, with the money he'd receive if it was pulled off, he'd get out sitting on a nice piece of change.

"...Who's comin'?"

His mind was so gone, Dino almost didn't catch Slim's question. "Oh, yeah my daughter," he said as they made it through the fence.

Slim was smiling and striding like a new man. "Damn, I haven't been this nervous in a long time."

"When's the last time you had a visit?"

"Almost ten years," he replied. "I mean, this woman don' changed my life."

The two men made it to the corridor that led to visiting. After knocking, they waited until an officer came to let them in.

"We're here for visiting," Dino said.

The officer was one of the new transfers. He was a young white kid with the name tag *PRATT*. He let them in. "Do you have your I.D.'s?"

Both Slim and Dino pulled them out.

"Okay, follow me."

Officer Pratt escorted them to a small room where they were stripped out. Once they were both completely naked, they were inspected for any contraband.

"Lift your nuts… dick… turn…"

Both men placed their hands on the wall.

"Spread your cheeks… drop and cough… Okay, put your clothes in the locker. What size jumpsuit?"

Dino said, "Four-X."

At the USP level, visitation for inmates called for them to wear jumpsuits and jellie slippers for their feet. Slim had to try on multiple jumpsuits since he wasn't used to going to visits. Finally, he found a 4X and size 13 slippers.

"Okay," Pratt began. "If you haven't been to visit, there's one kiss and hug at the beginning and end of your visit. No petting, kissing or touching during the visit. Make sure you…"

Dino spared the young officer some time. "We got'chu. We're out here all the time."

Pratt nodded. "Well, follow me."

Slim was rubbing his palms together.

Dino laughed. "So are you gonna kiss her champ?"

"I told her I was," he said smoothing his goatee and eyebrows.

The officer unlocked the door to the main visiting room and let them in. Dino began looking for his daughter the second

129

he stepped through the door. He saw her sitting next to the vending machines.

"Make sure you take your IDs to the desk," they were told.

Slim was looking around as he followed behind Dino to the desk.

"Do you see her?"

"Nah."

Dino handed his ID to the female officer working the desk. She checked his name on her clipboard. "Your visit is over there."

He nodded. "Thanks. Alright Slim."

"Alright…" he replied.

Dino made it over to his daughter. At 19 years old, she had grown to be a fine young lady. He was so proud of her. "Look at you," he said as she stood to hug him.

"Hey daddy."

The sitting arrangements were for the inmates to sit facing their visitor. So Dino sat, smiling and taking in his beautiful child. "How was your drive?"

"It was cool," she replied.

Dino saw a quick movement in his peripheral and realized it was Slim. His partner was a row in front of him to his left. His visitor was sitting there with a strange expression on her face.

Slim stood. "You're a what?" He was obviously upset.

Dino's daughter was also looking.

The woman with Slim was pleading. "Baby, sit down and let me explain."

Dino couldn't help but pay attention to the chick who came to see Slim. Dressed casual, her 12 inch weave was curled perfectly and heavy make-up coated her face. She looked like she really got dressed up to see him. So why was he upset?

That's when his partner got loud, drawing everyone's attention.

"Man, you got me fucked up!" Then he stormed to the officer's desk.

"You know him, daddy?"

Dino said, "Yeah, he's in my unit. That's a good dude. He just met that girl. It's their first time on visit."

"So… so, he didn't know she was a man?"

Turning, he looked at the woman who came to visit Slim. She was sitting there with her hands to her face, embarrassed. "That's a man?"

"Yep," his daughter confirmed. "A transgender."

Dino just shook his head. He couldn't believe it.

2

"So she was fucking him?" Alexis asked in pure awe.

Her and Erin were sitting in the Officers Mess Hall enjoying lunch together. The fight between Lt. Frost and Ted was the gossip amongst officers. Of course Alexis was behind on the scoop so her friend was trying to catch her up. "I just can't believe they're still walking around here like nothing ever happened."

Alexis agreed. "I would've brought my gun and waited until his ass pulled up if he would've kicked my ass like that. Was the pussy that good?"

"Was the dick that good? That's what I wanna know."

Alexis looked at her friend.

"What? I'm just sayin'! That bitch got dudes fightin', makin' her family and son look crazy."

"I forgot Adam was their son. They got all sorts of problems."

Leon, Hal, and a few other officers entered the lounge quieting the girls. The men walked over and spoke. While the rest continued to the counter for some food, Leon stayed back to speak with Alexis.

"So," he began. "What's the latest?"

She looked at him. "You tell us."

"Yeah," came Erin. "Word is y'all are plottin' on jumpin' the LT."

He laughed. "Fuck naw! Ted's my boy but I'm not boxin' with Chuck Norris behind some tail."

Alexis pouted her lips. "So you wouldn't fight to defend my honor?"

His eyes glossed over. Then he smiled. "Well, maybe for you sexy."

Erin just shook her head.

"So," he continued. "How about you come with me to the casino this weekend?"

Giving him a dumbfounded look Alexis said, "Casino? Baby, I get money. Not gamble it away. So the answer will be no."

Leon was taken back. "Damn, like that?"

"Yeah, so call me when you're going to Jamaica or on a shopping spree," she replied as if insulted by his offer.

"I heard that," Erin said giving her a high five.

In medical…

Nurse Frost had just closed her afternoon pill line and was ready to sit down and take a break. The last few days had been hectic and she was to the point where she was becoming numb to the situation. Grabbing a bag of chips out of the vending machine for her lunch, she retreated to the nurse's lounge to watch some TV and relax.

"Hey Ma."

The sound of her son's voice made her look up. "Adam… Hey, what are you doing down here?"

"I just wanted to see you," he said. Ever since he moved into his own place, they hadn't seen much of each other. "Can we talk?"

She nodded. "Yeah, come sit down."

Adam took a seat next to her on a plastic cushioned chair. "I was trying to call you the last few days to see how things have been."

"The same," she replied. "After all that shit in the parking lot, Richard's been staying at a motel."

"Have you spoken to Gibbs?"

"Actually, I've spoken to Ted every day since. He's a big boy."

"I heard he kicked his ass good."

Nurse Frost grimaced. "Yeah, you know Richard. I just wish I could figure out a way to get rid of his ass."

With it out in the open, Adam turned and looked at his mother. He long knew she was tired of his stepfather and he honestly wanted the same thing. "When you say get rid of him... what do you mean exactly?"

She gave him a look. "You know exactly what I mean."

Adam was silent in thought. Then he asked, "If... something... let's say, were to happen to him. What's in it for you?"

Taking a chip out the bag and putting it in her mouth, she savored the taste before responding. "His life insurance policy is for three-hundred and eighty thousand dollars."

The words spoken left both of them in deep thought.

While Nurse Frost and her son plotted the situation, Warden Maddox was having his own personal meeting. Standing in the center of his office, Lieutenant Frost, Captain McDaniels and Ted listened to their superior as he addressed the elephant in the room.

"I will not tolerate that kind of behavior at our workplace," Maddox said vehemently. "Richard, I've been knowing you for years but I was so embarrassed it took all my energy not to have you arrested."

The LT stood at attention, not saying a word.

The Warden continued. "We were all sent here to operate this prison with professionalism and efficiency. Fighting in our parking lot isn't the way and that high school behavior is out of place."

"But respectfully, Warden," Frost said finally. "This prick has been sleeping with my wife."

"I don't give a shit if he's fucking your mother!" Maddox's face was as red as his hair. The Irish in him was coming out, full throttle. "Take that backyard brawl shit out there in the desert somewhere."

Up to that point, Ted had not said a word. He only stood there. His eyes were still discolored and other than the eight stitches above his left eye, he was cool.

"Now," Maddox turned to him. "I don't know how you guys were doing it in Lompoc, Officer Gibbs. This little game you're playin' has to stop. You're violating all sorts of conduct codes, and I can have you transferred to the other side of the states behind this. Is that what you want?"

He shook his head.

"Good. Now keep your dick in your pants and out of his wife. I don't need another incident like we encountered last year."

All men knew they were referring to the gunman in the tower.

"So am I clear?"

The two men looked at the warden and nodded their heads.

"Great. Let me see you shake on it."

Ted turned to the LT and shook his hand. In the back of his mind, he knew then and there that he'd find a way to get him back. He had to. His pride wouldn't let this slide.

Oblivious to the drama escalating amongst the federal officers, the convicts on the compound were dealing with their own issues. Caught in the routine of doing time many simply looked forward to knocking down another day in their bid. With the heat turning up, many found themselves retired to the housing units early.

Dino had spent a full three hours talking to his daughter. Just graduating high school, she spoke with him about her interests of leaving California for Howard University or Spellman. Her mother didn't want her to leave and didn't support the decision at all. He told his daughter he'd support whatever decision and it made her smile. She thanked him and promised to let him know what she'd decided to do as soon as she figured it out.

Dino had just over $25,000 saved up from the hustling he'd been doing with Asian Lee. His visit left him thinking more and more about the $100,000 Gordo offered. After returning from his visit, he went inside, took a shower and now he was on night yard speaking to Maniak about the proposition.

"Do you think it could be done?"

Maniak looked off towards the track around the football field. "Honestly, anything is possible. I'm just trying to figure

out how we're supposed to get his fat ass in an oatmeal bag."
Then he looked at Dino. "These Mexicans will try anything."

He agreed. "I think he's crazy too. I can't stop thinking about how it may be possible, especially how easy we got it comin' in."

"I say we think some more on it. I mean, although it sounds way out, a hundred racks is enough to make a nigga wonder."

While the two of them spoke, they saw Asian Lee approach the fence on A-Yard. Dino got up. "Well, let me know what you come up with. I need to holler at Lee's mutha'fuckin' ass."

"Yeah, tell him it's about that time."

He nodded. "Fa'sho."

A rare cool, welcoming breeze came through blowing the heat waves that blanketed the yard. Dino crossed the basketball courts while a group of white boys played full court. He saw Bone and the Crips chilling on the stone built steps, used as a bleacher. "What's up y'all?"

They nodded.

Asian Lee leaned against the fence. "So, tell me some good news."

"Everything's gone," he reported. "My daughter came today, so I couldn't get word to you. When I got back, my boy told me he sold the last of the tobacco and weed."

"So, we're ready for another round?"

"Yep, whenever you're ready to have your people put it together. Maniak said the truck comes in next week."

Lee looked at his watch. "That means I gotta move fast."

"Real fast," he said, stepping a little closer Dino looked to enlighten his Asian friend. "Look, shits picking up. I say you have your people send two bags this time. That way we can turn this shit all the way up, and get the money while we can."

Lee didn't agree. "I don't wanna get greedy. We're getting enough for now. Plus, the object is to run out. That way we see the money. We don't want the product."

Dino left it alone. "Alright, if that's what you think." He didn't want his urge to make more money because of him going home corrupt his relationship with Lee. The man was making it all possible.

"How familiar are you with the white boy, Big Jake?" Lee asked.

The question caught him off guard. "Not real good. I mean, we've spoken at the little meetings and shit. You know prison politics. Why you askin'?"

"He's in my unit," Lee began. "About a week ago we had some words."

"About what?"

"If you ask me, he's jealous and wants in on the action. Those type of people I just don't trust."

This was an issue that he didn't need. Dino couldn't let anyone interfere with his main supplier, but he did not want to commit to an alliance to the Asians. "Why do you think that?"

Lee looked him square in the eye. "Money and business is what I know. I've brokered deals in million dollar suits as well as the ghetto alleys of Shanghai. When a man cannot get what he desires, he will use fear and intimidation as his first tactic. When that fails, he'll use other means. In our case, he'll either rat you out or manufacture a way to wipe you out."

That's when he explained what happened.

Dino caught his drift. He still tried to remain neutral, at least for now. "Well, until he makes another comment, or jumps out there, don't pay him no mind. I really don't believe he'll tell on you."

"Hmph… I wouldn't bet on it."

When the 7:30 p.m. indoor move was called, Dino took it inside with the majority of others. He found the unit much more noisy now that the 100 plus were moved in. As soon as he walked through the doors, Donnie approached him with a crooked smile on his face.

"Dog… man, you ain't tell me about Slim," he said in a whisper, trying hard not to laugh.

Dino shook his head. "Yeah, my boy got catfished. He was calling her.. him, boo and everything."

His young partners busted up laughing. "All this time? He never knew?"

"Man, Slim lost it in there. I mean, he went off, jumped up and bounced. My daughter told me it was a transgender. Trust me, he never knew."

"Ahh shit!"

Dino shushed him. "Come on now, I don't want to be the one to put it out there," he said. "I already feel bad I helped him write his bio for that pen pal website."

Donnie waved him off. "Man, niggas is already talkin' about it."

"What? Where's Slim now?"

Depression...

They say misery loves company and depression is in love with stress. Both can wound a man tremendously, especially one who's clinging onto life by a single thread.

The cell was cluttered with torn up scraps of letters, envelopes, and greeting cards stamped with lipstick kisses and perfume. Relics of a love that resurrected Slim's lost soul, which had been withering behind the federal prison walls. The visit crushed him, sending him back to his room in total anguish.

With a towel draped over the cell doors window, he stood in the darkness. Tears were rolling out of his eyes. All he could think about was the life sentence he was serving and all the bad luck he had. In his mind, God had shitted on him again, and was sitting in Heaven having a good ole laugh.

Well not any longer, he thought. *I'll be a fool no more.*

Slim took a step up on the metal toilet and turned his back to the wall. Above him was a vent where he fashioned a prison-styled noose made up of torn bed sheet strips, woven through the small holes. On another occasion, he flirted with the idea of hanging himself to end the nightmare he was living. Now he was going to finally go through with it.

Slipping his head through the loop, he tucked it under his neck. "I love you mother…"

The weight of his body fell downward causing his neck to snap instantly. He went into convulsions, kicking and thrashing in suspended air. His eyes rolled in the back of his head as he chocked and gagged. Until finally…

He thrashed no more.

3

The sound of the metal food slot latches being opened and closed echoed down the range, letting Champ know just how close the C.O.'s were to his cell. While the others in the SHU couldn't wait for their breakfast, he couldn't wait to get his hands on the officer that lied to him. It had been a week since he was told a Chaplin would come to see him. He still hadn't used the phone and this would make the day they were to bury his mother.

It was okay. He'd settle it his own way.

"Hey C.O!" someone called out. "You forgot the milk."

Laughter. "That's just too bad," one officer called out.

"Yeah, drink some water. It's good for you," came the other.

More laughter from the C.O.'s.

With his light off, Champ stood in the dark. The sun had not come up so no rays shone through his back window. The food slot next door to him opened, and he stepped to the door and saw the cart with a white officer pushing it. Officer Pratt was handing out trays, which was exactly what Champ hoped for.

"Service with a smile," Pratt told the inmates in the cell, before closing and locking the slot.

Champ kneeled down as the wheels to the cart squeaked in front of his cell. He got really low in front of the slot. The officer inserted his key and unlocked it, turning the flap down so he could place a tray inside it.

"Rise and shine Princess," Pratt called out as he looked into the dark cell.

Moving fast, Champ's hand shot out of the food slot, grabbing the officer by the wrist.

"Hey!" Pratt blurted.

With a vice grip, he broke the man's hand, sending him crumbling to his knees on the other side of the door. Champ pulled his whole arm into the cell with brute force, slamming his head against the door. Pratt's face was turned so he could see who it was. "Yeah bitch, you think I was gonna let you get away with lying to me?"

"Ahh!" Pratt called out in pain. "Let me go you bastard!"

His partner hit the deuces and grabbed his radio. "Officer down... attacked in the SHU... B-Range..." Then he yelled at Champ. "Let him go!"

However, Champ wasn't listening. With a firm lock on Pratt's arm, he twisted it, as he stood up. Now with it completely stretched out, he dropped his knee across the elbow, breaking it like a twig, the bone snapping with force.

"Ahh!"

Then he yanked the arm with force, slamming the officer's head banging against the door.

Boom! Boom! Boom!

"That's right!" Champ yelled. "Cry mutha'fucka! Let me hear you cry loud enough for my momma to hear yo' bitch ass way up in heaven."

The sound of jingling keys came as inmates and convicts on the SHU's range were now beating on cell doors and yelling.

"Get that punk! That's right DC!"

The ten men Tactical Response Team raced to their co-worker's aid, led by Lieutenant Frost. "Open this fucking door," he ordered.

The officer working alongside Pratt did just that. Once the cell door was opened, all hell broke loose.

Champ backed up to the far end of the cell. "That's right! Come get it!"

With his team behind him, Frost charged into the cell, stepping over a whimpering Officer Pratt. With massive strength, Champ swung haymaker fists, missing Frost but catching another officer clean, and dropping him. The miss left Frost an opening to land a sharp uppercut that dazed Champ enough for the others to rat pack him. He tried to wrestle them off but they were too much.

Karate chop blows, Hi-Tek boots, knees, and elbows assaulted Champ like a Rodney King beating. They kicked his head into the wall and bunk, leaving blood pouring from his head and nose. Until finally the hulk of a man wouldn't move.

He was knocked completely out.

The suicide committed by Slim didn't affect the institutions everyday operations at all. Though it left many shocked, the majority forgot it even occurred almost immediately.

Dino was a little messed up about it. He knew that Slim hated the fact that he had a life sentence but he never would've thought the man would commit suicide. It was the first at the facility but he'd seen it before; situations where guys lost their will to survive and gave up.

They let the system beat them of the time they had left on earth. It was a story many fell victim to.

Dino knew he had to stay focused. With his days being numbered, and his daughter eager for his return home, he set his mind on getting paid. There was no way he was going to get out of prison broke.

As soon as he got word to have Lee's people get their next shipment ready, the Asian set things in motion. Maniak and Bone were already waiting with money on standby from some of their homeboys. When the time came for the truck to arrive at the warehouse, Bone had Ty and Lil' B ready to go, while Maniak did his usual with the kitchen supervisor, Mr. Casey. Once the drop was made, Bone did his thing, and like clockwork, Dino gathered it all on his hot trash rounds.

It was the sweetest lick they'd ever put down and with Lee reconsidering doubling up this time, that meant more money to go around.

In B-Unit...

Joe-Joe was cleaning out his cell because the word was that another bus was coming, so he prepared to get a cellie. He didn't want one but he'd handle that when the time came. Until then he sorted out all the property he'd just picked up from R and D.

When he saw Ms. Green switching her thick hips down the tier searching cells, something told him she was going to go into his. So once he was finished putting away all his pictures, he sat his photo album on the bunk, and stepped out just as she made it to his door.

"How you doin' Ms. Green?" he asked with a smile.

Alexis twisted her lips. "Hmph... boy wha'chu up to?"

"Boy? Baby girl, I'm all man. Straight up," he replied in a non-threatening tone.

"That's what y'all all say." She stepped inside his cell and started closing the door.

He just shook his head. He really liked her style.

Petey Moe came up the steps. "Yo, I got at Jinx and he said the Crip nigga got ounces of that kush for twenty-five hun'ned."

He shook his head. "That's too much," he said with his voice lowered. Meanwhile, his eyes stayed on her in his cell.

"That's what I said. These niggas don't wanna see anybody get on."

"That's why we gotta get our own shit poppin'. These Cali dudes all about they self."

Turning and looking, Petey Moe said, "Damn, you got fat ass up in yo' shit lookin' all at your pictures."

Joe-Joe took a peek and saw Ms.Green sitting on his bunk, looking at his collection of photos. Not only were there flicks of him and his boys getting money, all the flashy cars and jewels he once had, but there was also a bunch of pictures from all the females he had in his life. Flicks of them in lingerie, posing in erotic positions. Females that made her look average.

He shook his head. "Yeah, she's a trip."

"Well, I'm about to hop on this phone," Petey said going back down the stairs. "You know a bus comin'."

"I know. We might be gettin' a cellie."

"Shit, I'm try'nah move mine in before that."

"Who you try'nah move in there?"

143

His homeboy grinned. "You know me."

Joe-Joe laughed. He knew his homeboy was burnt out, hinting at moving in the homosexual.

After about ten more minutes, he looked back inside his cell only to see Ms.Green still in her same spot on his bunk. He opened the door and to his surprise, she did not move. "Uh... are you comfortable?"

With the photo album in her lap, she just turned the page. "Is this you?" she asked pointing at a picture of him standing next to a Rolls Royce Phantom.

"Yeah."

She simply nodded. "That's your car?"

"Yep one of them."

She looked up. "Oh, you were ballin'?"

He did not respond as she turned a page. Joe-Joe saw her admiring all the photos of him in Jamaica, in clubs flashing money and hugging exotic women. Then she turned to all the pictures he had of the chicks he knew.

"Damn," she said of a thick red bone. "She got more ass than me."

At first, he could not believe his ears. However, he was not one to be shy or intimidated, so he replied. "Almost... but not quite. Her ass ain't as nice and firm as yours."

She played as if she did not hear him. After looking at a few more, she closed it and stood up. "All them girls," she began. "You just a playa, huh? Got all of 'em fightin' and shit behind you I bet."

"Nah ma', they just down for a nigga. That is all. I kept it real with them and they're doing the same for me," he smiled and said. "They know it ain't any other like me. I'm the last of a dyin' breed."

Moving past him in the small cell, Alexis brushed her soft body against him. "Yeah, you's a playa."

Then she left his cell.

It was that moment that Joe-Joe decided he would try his hand with her. If it failed, he figured at least he gave it a shot.

THE WALL

It was time for shift change and officers were coming to work, carrying their Jansport backpacks and bottled water...
Ted came through the doors of the administration building just as Nurse Frost was leaving. As soon as he saw her, he knew she wanted to talk.

"Can you spare five minutes?" she asked.

Ever since the incident, he'd spoken to her but tried to keep his distance for his jobs sake. "Listen I think we should wait..."

"Just five minutes," she said cutting him off.

He nodded. "Alright, let's go to the breakroom."

The two were happy when they found the breakroom empty. Nurse Frost entered behind him and closing the door, she stood next to it, holding the handle so no one could get in.

"Ted, I'm done," she told him.

"You and the LT?"

"Yes, I'm ready to move on." Her eyes were hard and serious. "And I want to be with you."

For a moment, he didn't know what to say. Then he rubbed her cheek. "Suga, are you..."

"Yes, I'm sure," she finished. "I'm tired and it's obvious it's over between us." Leaning close she looked him square in the eyes. "Can I trust you with something?"

"Of course."

"After what he did to you, babe, I want his ass dead." Her words were hard and unwavering.

He laughed. "Listen, I know you're upset. Shit, I am too. But-"

"But my ass, Ted. If anything happens to him, I have a life insurance policy for three-hundred grand." She let her words sink in. "That's a whole lot of money to start a new life with."

Ted saw she wasn't joking at all. She didn't know, but he had thoughts of his own. "So what do you think we should do?"

With a devious look on her face, Nurse Frost said, "Well, a lot of things can happen to an officer in prison. Who says *we* have to do anything." She emphasized the word we.

He caught her drift.

Someone came to the door, shaking the handle. "Is somebody in there?"

Nurse Frost gave him one last knowing look before she let go of the handle. She opened the door and smiled. "Hey."

It was Erin. "Uh… I hope I didn't interrupt anything Mrs. Frost."

"Oh, no," she replied. "We were just leaving and call me Tina, please."

Erin smiled. "Okay."

Ted headed out of the breakroom with his lover behind him. He didn't want to draw any more attention so once he came to the metal detectors, he simply turned and said, "I'll think about what you said."

She mouthed a 'thank you' and headed towards the doors to leave.

It was an hour into his shift working A-Unit and Ted couldn't help but think about Nurse Frost's proposition. Also how she was insisting their co-workers refer to her by her first name. He knew it was no secret that they were having an affair, not to mention the fight between him and her husband.

$300,000. The amount kept popping up in his head. There was no doubt in his mind about him wanting revenge for what happened to him. Shit, he was still bruised with a black eye and sore all over. Kill him for it? That is when a thought came to him. Sitting up quickly, Ted logged onto the computer and looked up an inmate.

Anything I can do to repay you… anybody gets out of line… he heard offered over and over in his mind. *Let me know, I'll take care of it.*

Finally, he found the person he was looking for. Jake Calhoun also known as *The Butcher*. Multiple life sentences for mayhem and murder. Ted scrolled through the man's pre-sentence report and saw he wasn't a rat, highly aggressive and loved violence. He did 3 years in Juvenile Hall for assault and battery, beating a man with a baseball bat.

Sitting back in his seat, Ted contemplated the thoughts going through his mind. They were crazy, but it was highly possible.

Very possible.

EPISODE 5
CROSSING THE LINE

1

The basketball court on B-Yard was packed. With more new convicts at the facility, the league basketball games got underway. There were ten teams with full rosters. Players from all over with the skills to perform. Being the institution was new, it made it more exciting having all the equipment available: shot clock, new balls, nets, scorecards, referee jerseys and whistles. It didn't take long to assemble the officials or teams. Most of the convicts looked forward to the season as it was their way of doing time.

Maniak was sitting on the stone bleachers talking to Bone. The Bloods and Crips flanked them as the two O.G's discussed the business they had amongst them. With Dino making it possible for all of them to make money, they sought ways to capitalize off the product they had.

Meanwhile, the GD's, Vice Lords, Dirty South, D.M.V and others, grouped up around the court to watch the first game of the season. The teams tipping off both boasted two centers, a 6'9", white boy and a 6'10" black dude from Chicago.

It looked to be a good match up. With both teams center court the ref performed the jump ball, which ended with the 6'9" player's team winning the tip. The chain of events that followed produced an alley-oop dunk by a cat just over six feet tall.

The crowd went wild.

Bone continued his point to Maniak as if the action on the court didn't exist. "I think we should bust all that shit down and get as much as we can," he said just amongst them. "You never know when this shit will be over wit'."

Maniak listened to the man's point before adding his insight. "I feel you but that's a lot to be busting down. We also wanna get that bread out to the streets fast enough to pay for the next batch comin'. That nigga Dino's about to go home, so if

149

we're gonna take over his position with Lee then we gotta get that bread up."

The two stopped speaking when they saw a player on the court drive into the lane, jump for a lay-up and get hacked hard by the 6'10" center.

The ref blew the whistle. "Foul!"

6'10" barked at the ref. "What? I ain't touch him."

The ref was a short, stocky, light skinned man from Texas named Red. "Yeah, you touched him. You damn near tore his whole head off."

6'10" waved him off. "Cheatin' ass mutha'fucka."

"I got'cho mutha'fucka, you big soft-bitch ass nigga," Red said not backing down.

"Man, I'll knock you out!"

The exchange of words brought cats on the sidelines to attention. Maniak sat watching as the GD's braced for any type of aggression. With Spike as their rep, the group made sure none of the Texas guys made any moves. Everyone knew knives were definitely in rotation on the yard.

Red was about to react when another ref named Lou stepped in between them. "Come on y'all," the older black guy said. "Let's play ball and leave all that fussin' alone."

Surprisingly, that's all that was needed. The big man separated himself while Red gave the scorer's table his jersey number.

"This shit's crazy," Bone said. "I bet the league don't make it a good week before somebody get stabbed."

Maniak agreed. "I already know."

The sight of a small group moving towards the court drew their attention. Bone's homeboy, Tray, leaned over and whispered something in his ear, nodding towards an individual in the group.

"Aye, you see ole boy right there," he said.

Maniak looked in the direction Bone was referring to.

"Yeah, what about him?"

"His name is Petey Moe. He's from DC. My boy says them niggas is askin' bout some zips of kush. Him and his homeboy Joe-Joe."

He had gotten word that the DC boys were trying to get on. "Is you try'nah fuck wit' them?"

Bone shook his head. "Nah. Like I said, I'm try'nah see all mine. Plus, them niggas be havin' too much shit wit' them."

The rumor of DC dudes being ruthless, cut throat, and bad business was something Maniak had heard for years. His personal experience didn't attest to that. Bone's outlook was his own, and he did not argue it. "Well, I'll let an ounce go for fifteen-hundred. But I'm only doin' wire transactions. No stamps."

Tray looked at Maniak and asked, "Do you want me to put the word out there?"

"Yeah, you can."

On the other side of the court...

Petey Moe stood in the group mixed with DC, Maryland and Virginia dudes. None of their homeboys were playing but they wanted to let the other convicts see their faces. With Butta finished fashioning knives for all them, each man looked ready for whatever their new home brought their way.

"Why ain't Joe-Joe come out?" Butta asked.

"You know that nigga... Slim be on his work out shit. Oh Iron Man ass nigga," Petey Moe said.

Jinx strolled over from a small group of cats he was talking to, shaking his head.

"What the fucks wrong wit' you," Petey Moe asked recognizing the frustration on his partner's face.

"These niggas gon' make me take shit to another level."

His comment made several in their group look back towards the men he was referring to.

"What, are they trippin?" Butta asked.

Jinx rubbed his head and exhaled a long sigh. "Nah, they owe the table six-hundred, between all of 'em."

"Oh yeah?" Petey Moe reached underneath his shirt for his brand new razor sharp knife. "Is they bucking'?"

"Hell nah!" Jinx replied. "Bitch ass niggas don't want it. They just need to get my money right, that's all."

"That poker shit be havin' yo' ass stressed the fuck out," Butta laughed.

"Yeah, but the hustle don't stop."

All around the basketball court and yard, small groups like this congregated. Their discussions ranged from compound business, to prison politics, recent incidents and issues concerning their cars. The institution was up in numbers and the majority were still getting settled in. For the rest, it was no different from the last prison.

Seen one. Seen 'em all.

In B-Unit...

Joe-Joe had just finished a serious workout and now he was letting the hot sprays from the showerhead soothe his body. With an 8 inch knife hanging near on the cloth hook he let the water flow over his head, and through his dreads. Once he rinsed his hair thoroughly, he cut the water off and stepped to the plastic partitioned, where his towel and clothes were.

That's when he saw her staring at him from the second tier. From that angle, she could see directly into the shower. He smiled and took a step back, putting his wet and chiseled naked body in clear view. He didn't know how long she'd been watching but if it was a show she was looking for, he'd give it to her.

Alexis twisted her lip up playfully and stood up from her resting position on the rail. Then turning, she continued down the tier.

Damn, he thought watching her. *All that ass... Ain't nobody bangin' that shit out.* Joe-Joe laughed as he finished drying himself off. He had a feeling deep down inside that he was going to knock her. When he did, he planned on turning the tide in the favor of him and his homeboys.

In the back hallway of the Unit Team's offices...

Dino was finishing his orderly duties. He'd mopped the hallway, emptied the garbage, cleaned the windows, and helped his case manager, Mr. Carson, move a desk out of one of the offices. Once his counselor, Ms. White, was finished using the staff's bathroom, he got the spray bottles and comet cleanser out of the utility room. After he finished in there he'd be done.

Opening the bathroom, Dino stepped inside. "What the...." Instantly he grabbed his nose. The stench of shit hit him like a ton of bricks. "My goodness lady, what the hell you eat?"

Stepping to the toilet, he saw brown splattered fecal matter all over the back of the seat. It was as if she miss fired, as the shit burst from her butthole. He gagged at the sight, firing rounds of chemical cleanser from the spray bottle.

"Nasty ass bitch," he muttered. He hated his job but it was the perk of having such a sweet stash spot that he loved. So gritting his teeth he managed through it, using the whole spray bottle and can of comet on the job.

It took twenty minutes but finally Dino was able to bring the bathroom back to a civil standard. Now that that was done he needed to handle one more thing before he wrapped up. So after taking a quick peek down the hall, he looked to see if anyone was coming. When he saw all was clear he moved quickly, stepping onto the toilet seat and reaching up into the bathroom's ceiling.

"Hey Peterson..."

Dino snatched his arm down at the sound of Mr. Carson's voice. When he looked, the man was standing right there in the doorway.

Back inside the unit...

Alexis was in the office talking to Erin on the phone. She was so into their conversation that she did not see Leon standing in the doorway. "Girl, let me call you back."

"Okay," Erin replied.

Smiling from ear to ear, Leon took a seat. "Hey stranger, what's been up with you?"

"Nothing much," she replied. "Same ole shit. Workin' these shifts."

He nodded. "I've been trying to call you. Why haven't you returned any of my messages?"

"Like I said, I've been busy." Her response held no remorse or feeling.

Leon was confused. "Look, I don't know what I did that got'chu actin' all funny on me..."

She cut him off. "I'm not acting funny, Leon. I think you're getting a little too serious."

"Serious?"

"Yeah, you're taking this a little too serious. Like I said. I mean damn, we kicked it and had a little fun. Now every time I turn around I got you all up in my ass." Alexis gave him a cold stare. "We fucked Leon... what else do you want?"

At first he just sat there as if hurt by her comment, then he just smiled. "You know what? You're right. I should've known your stripper ass couldn't resist a dollar and some good dick."

Her face dropped.

"Yeah, you thought no one knew about you, huh?" Now it was his turn to give her the cold stare. "Bitch, how you think you could pose in all those ass magazines and take all those Instagram pics in the strip club and no one find out who you really were? Yeah... Miss Candy Licka! You'z a hoe outta Houston and once a hoe always one."

Leon stood and removed a twenty dollar bill from his pocket.

"Here hoe," he said tossing it in the air, sending it fluttering down upon her. "That's the last time I'll make it rain on ya. Take that and buy yourself a life."

Alexis sat dumbfounded as Leon exited the office. Her mind was clouded and she felt embarrassed at the fact her past was exposed. What she didn't know was just outside the office door...

Joe-Joe had just finished using the microwave when he heard the outburst. Stepping to the side, he held his bowl of oatmeal listening as the officer cursed her out.

Stripper?

Then the dude stormed out like he was hurt at the fact.

I knew there was something about her, Joe-Joe thought as he headed back to his cell. *I knew that bitch was about that dough.*

Back to the staff bathroom...

Dino froze at the sight of Mr. Carson. "Uh... this damn drop ceiling fell so I was trying to put it back." His mind couldn't think of nothing else to say. If he didn't say something he was surely cooked. There was a new federal indictment up there.

"It fell?" The case manager looked crazy. "Here, let me see."

Stepping down from the toilet, Dino moved out the way. Mr. Carson took his place, reaching up and lifting the ceiling's square sheet back into place. The whole while Dino held his breath.

"There, that should do it," he said stepping down.

Dino just looked at him.

"Are you finished yet? I need to take you back to the unit."

"Uh... yeah, I already hit everything," he replied pointing to different areas of the bathroom to toss the focus elsewhere. He held the spray bottle up. "I just need to put this back in the closet."

"Alright."

As Dino moved to the utility closet, Mr. Carson took his keys off the latch on his belt and locked the bathroom door. He put up the bottle and the case manager took him back to the unit. For Dino, it was a close call but he was so thankful he wiggled his way out of that.

It was too close for comfort.

2

The institutions workout room was state of the art. With all sorts of equipment for strength and conditioning, it provided the staff with the means to stay fit. Mirrored walls and flat screen TV's made working out motivational and entertaining. Being the majority of the staff didn't use the room, it was the perfect place for Lieutenant Frost to find peace.

Sweating profusely, the LT swung kicks and combination punches into the weight bag. Each blow he struck sent the bag swinging on its chains, left and right. Bare foot, the mat beneath him gave the best platform for angles and stances. Not one to slack on his training, Frost kept this fit by pushing the limits. He was thirty minutes in and hadn't lost a step.

Whap! Whap! Came a double kick.

Captain McDaniels entered the room and headed right for the LT. He didn't want to interrupt the workout so he watched patiently until the man finished his set.

Frost came off the mat. His Under Armor workout shirt and shorts were soaked. "Cap'…"

McDaniels nodded. "Rich… if I'dah known you were coming in today I would've went a few rounds with you."

A vet himself, Frost knew his Captain's marine training wasn't up to par. "You could've used it."

He patted his newly acquired gut. "Yeah, I know. Only if the guys could see me now."

Not really in the mood for talking, the LT grabbed the bottle of Gatorade and took a long drink. Then he grabbed a towel. "Honestly, I came in on my day off to relax and clear my mind."

"Well… I saw you in here and figured I'd have a word with you."

"About what?" The last thing he wanted to discuss was the issue concerning the parking lot fight. What he heard next caught him by surprise.

"I just want you to know I support what you represent, one hundred percent." The Captain's voice held extreme adoration. "These playboy dipshits come to work corrections, not having the slightest respect for morals and code."

He agreed. "No honor for our brotherhood."

"Exactly!" McDaniels shook his head. "Boy, you're a better man than me. I would've killed his ass, flat out."

The LT laughed a bit. "Then I would've been in a worse off position. No, I'm gonna do what's best for me. This won't be my fall. That slut can never be my weakness. It's been a long time comin', Mac. The divorce can't be prevented."

The Captain understood completely. "I just want you to know you have my full support."

Frost acknowledged his appreciation and went for the showers. While standing under the hot water, he cried silently to himself. He wanted to kill Ted so bad, he felt it in his bones.

Early morning on the yard...

It was the first recreation move of the morning and everyone came out to enjoy the rare cool temperature. The handball and basketball courts were full of players and fitness groups.

Dino made his way out so he could discuss some business. Since he began making moves, he intended to reach out to the reps of other cars when the time was right. He knew he couldn't look out for all of them at once. So he made his decision to speak to those he'd been there the longest with.

His first stop was to holler at Tito, who was over the Latin Kings. Sending word for the man to meet him, Dino extended the offer to supply the man with tobacco, kush, and meth at a reasonable price. After negotiating prices and a payment system, Tito hopped onboard.

Another satisfied customer.

The next person Dino went to speak to was Spike. The GD's were out every morning, paired up in groups of six, working out. When Dino pulled up on him, Spike separated himself from the group he was instructing.

"I won't take up all your time."

"Ain't no problem," Spike assured him. "What's up?"

"Look," Dino said lowering his voice. "I got a few things poppin' and I wanted to extend an offer to you."

Getting straight to the specifics, Dino gave him prices and deals that would enable Spike to look out for his homeboys in a way they could all eat. He explained how he wanted to be paid and where to transfer the money.

"Yeah, we can definitely do some business," Spike said. "The Western Union isn't a problem either." He looked at the growing number of GD's working out. "This will be cool for them to get some money. I ain't really trippin'."

Dino nodded. "Well, figure out exactly what you're try'nah get and I'll be out here tonight."

"Okay, fa'sho," Spike said returning to his group. "And thanks too."

"No prob."

Once he left Spike, Dino's next stop was to holler at Gator. Although the man had been worrying himself to death about whether or not the DC boys were tripping on him or not, Dino knew that Gator was really a good guy.

"Makin' money is my thang!" Gator said smiling a mouth full of gold teeth. "Plus, we just got sum'mo homeboys from the South... Let me see what I can put together."

"Alright, well get at me."

"I sure will."

As Dino made his way across the yard, he saw his Paisa partner, Gordo, waving at him by the fence. He almost forgot about the man with all that was going on. So changing course, he headed over there.

"Where have you been, Dino?"

He smiled. "Trying to get some things in motion. I don't have a lot of time left so I'm doing my best to get ready for them streets."

Giving him a knowing look, the Mexican said, "Let me help you by putting a hundred-grand in an account somewhere. Don't think I was joking one bit."

"Oh, I took you seriously."

"Did you?" Gordo was all business now. "Listen, my reason for wanting that phone was to contact my people in Mexico, some of my trusted associates. They told me that although my Cartel has moved forward with different leadership, if I return I'm sure to resume my position. That's why I need you. Once I'm out, there will be no return for me."

"But how will you get to Mexico?"

The man smiled. "Trust me, we've been traveling through desert and back ways to America for years. That will not be a problem. I'm conditioned for it."

Dino thought of the heat Death Valley presented. "Well, I still need to iron a few things out with my people. We need to figure out if it's even possible."

"Just remember, anything is possible my friend. Anything."

On A-Yard...

The growing group of Whiteboys congregated at tables surrounding the track and football field. Big Jake and his new road dog, Dingo, sat on the bleachers, beneath the shedding. Jake only came out because he wanted to meet the three Irish dudes who had just arrived. Their case was legendary, as they made up the three contract killers known as Slaughterhouse. With over 250 documented murders, ranging from dismemberment, execution style shootings, hangings, arsons, and drownings, there was even more suspected deaths no one ever found out about.

Jake's type of crew.

Bald with green four leaf clover tattoos on top of their heads, the three white guys mingled with their new comrades.

"It feels good to finally get out that fucking county jail," the one named Lucky expressed. He was the oldest of the three at 39.

The other two were Chris and Jason O'Leary. They were brothers born in Ireland, but raised in the city of Boston. Jason was known as the brutal of the two, preferring deaths ending in torture. Chris was the oldest at 30. He loved guns and explosives.

"So Big Jake," Chris said looking around. "How long have you been here?"

"Close to two years now, I guess."

"And you?" he asked next of Dingo.

"Oh, I just got here."

Jason was once standing, now he sat. "Has anybody escaped from here? The place looks like a concrete fortress."

Jake laughed. "It is! But no, no one has ever escaped."

Lucky pointed at the tower. "Is that the infamous Tower of Doom?"

The phrase emerged after the psychotic officers shooting spree. No one on the yard had been referring to it as that. The more buses pulled up, Big Jake was beginning to hear it. "Yeah that's it."

"That was a sick fuck," Chris offered.

His brother had a different opinion. "I would've loved to be out here when it happened."

"Were you?" Lucky asked the big man.

"Actually, I had just went inside the unit. Thirty seconds slower and I could've probably been a victim."

Switching subjects, Jason looked to explain why he asked Jake about escaping. "I got two life sentences to figure out how in the hell to get out of here."

Chris roughly palmed his brother's fuzzy baldhead. "You couldn't find your way out of a wet paper bag."

"Plus, we're in the middle of nowhere," came Lucky.

Big Jake thought about the possibilities of escape many times. He felt like Lucky. "At this level of security, it would be better to relocate. This place is the first of its kind." He pointed in the sky. There, in the immediate area, a drone flew. "That's a first, anywhere."

They all looked.

"Why do they call this place ADX?" Dingo asked curiously. "All I saw when we pulled up is the compound, surrounded by a fifty-foot wall."

Chris nodded. "I was thinking the same thing."

"Well," Big Jake began. "The word is the ADX facility to this place is underneath the institution. They call it Area 52."

"Beneath the compound?" Jason had never heard of such a prison.

Dingo started looking at the grass on the field. "So there's supposed to be inmates in cells down there?"

Jake shrugged. "It's just what they say."

Inside B-Unit…

It was chest day for Joe-Joe and he went extra hard. He put together a routine mixed with crawl out burpies, Navy Seal push-ups wide and diamond, then capped it all off with 300 dips using the treadmill. When he finished, he was blown up like a blimp, with muscles and veins poking out everywhere.

For days now, he had been thinking about what he heard concerning Ms. Green. He could tell that the other officer hurt her feelings by how she'd been moping around. She just wasn't herself. Normally, when they crossed paths, she'd say something slick. Not anymore. He needed to find a way to capitalize off of what he knew, but there was no way to get close to her while she was in this state of mind.

Joe-Joe was on his way from the shower when he saw her come out of the cell next to his. Looking to break the ice, he gave her a head nod and said, "What's up? You lookin' like you ready to put that knife in somebody around here."

She gave a weak smile. "Nah, but don't be surprised if I lost it," she replied.

Standing there with his shower shoes, towel and wash cloth, Joe-Joe figured he'd jump out on a limb. He opened his cell door. "Aye look, check this out." Then he stepped inside.

Curious to see what he wanted, she followed behind him. "Check what out?"

He turned to face her, tossing his things onto his bunk. "Alexis, right?" he asked.

She put a hand on her hip. "Boy, I ain't got time…"

He held up a hand. "First off, I told you about that boy shit, Miss Lady. You talkin' to a real nigga here. I ain't no rat and have always shown you nothing but respect, right?"

His tone stopped her short. "Yeah, it's Alexis. Why?"

Here goes nothin', he thought. "You know, I've been down a while and I've seen a lot of shit. But I've never seen anything like that sucka shit that pussy ass punk pulled on you the other day." He looked dead in her eyes as he spoke.

Alexis tried to play stupid. "What are you talkin' about?"

Joe-Joe shook his head. "Come on… I was at the microwave when bitch boy got all in his body behind you checkin' him. All that shit he was talking 'bout."

She looked shocked. "You heard…"

He held up a hand. "Baby, I'm the last to judge you. Like I said, I'm a real nigga from the streets and I can see you're a real bitch. You've got a job now with mutha'fuckas who's not cut from the same cloth as us." His voice grew very sensitive as he spoke. "Even though I'm on this side of the fence, me and you are one and the same."

Something about how he looked at her was comforting.

He continued. "We're go getters. That cat, I've seen his kind many of times before. He can't handle a strong woman. He lashed out and got verbally abusive. Don't let that shit get to you, baby girl. Keep getting that cake out of these fools. Do you! And hold your head up while you do it."

At first she didn't know how to respond. Then she grew defensive. "So, you think you know me?"

He laughed. "Are you really gonna play that game right now?"

Just when she was about to protest, a short Hispanic man came to the cell and interrupted their conversation.

"Hey lady, I'm trying to get my ID back for this iron," he said in a frustrated voice.

Before she could say anything Joe-Joe moved past her and snapped. "Aye man, don't you see we talkin'!" His face was twisted in anger. "Take yo' ass downstairs by the office, and wait until she gets there."

The dude seemed confused.

"What, you gotta problem?" Joe-Joe was now advancing upon him.

The guy started backing up. "No, no man, my bad." Then he turned and went down the steps.

Turning back into the cell, Joe-Joe unconsciously pulled the door closed and moved past Alexis. "Now, where were we?"

She just looked at him like he was crazy. "Oh my gosh, you didn't have to do that."

"What?" He shook his head and gave her a stern look. "Listen, that's what I'm try'nah tell you. These mutha'fuckas, police and inmates, they not like you and me. They bitches! You gotta check a bitch, straight up. I know you wanna keep yo' job. You try'nah get paid. But once you let these sucka's dictate how you do you, that's when you become a bitch like them."

Alexis listened and finally said, "You know what, I feel you."

"Do you? Because I don't think you do," he said with laughter. "That dude was callin' you all sorts of ho's and shit. He didn't give a fuck that y'all were at work. All that professional shit they preach to y'all is just talk. The sooner you recognize this ain't nothin' but a job, like Mickey D's, the better. And if you fuckin' wit' the right ones, it's a lot you can do with it."

Now it was her turn to laugh. "So that's what this is all about? Makin' a dollar?"

"Fuckin' right! Tell me, how much you make a month? Five grand? Six? What?"

She just remained silent.

He shook his head. "You's a bad bitch. I bet you've seen a month's check in one night before."

The compliment flattered her.

"Yeah, I knew it." Pulling the rubber band out of his hair, he let his dreads fall. Then he took off his shirt.

Alexis grew startled. "I think…"

"What?" he said suddenly. "Girl… you ain't got shit to worry about. These niggas know what it is, even if we was on something."

"I don't need nobody thinkin'—"

He stopped her, and said, "Look, this ain't nothin' but a job. Remember that. I can see you're smart. Don't let these people brainwash you into becoming a slave who would sacrifice their life for pennies. Now that you got this job, make the most out of it. And when I say that, I don't mean fuckin' with these tender dick dudes either."

She looked him up and down as he stood there half-naked. "Well, what do you mean?"

Joe-Joe took one step closer to her. Then looking her square in the eye he said, "Today is your Friday. When you come back, if you're really interested, I'll let you know exactly what I mean. And if you're wit' it, trust me, I'll make sure that little check they payin' you will be crumbs compared to what I got to offer."

For a moment, she just stared deeply into his eyes as if in disbelief. She had never met a man with so much aggression and confidence in her entire life.

Never.

3

The Officer Mess Hall was serving hamburgers and fries, along with a cool environment to sit and relax. It had been a while since the three friends had enjoyed time together. So Hal, Ted, and Leon looked to catch up on the latest, while milking the clock of some free money.

"You're the only one that doesn't seem to have any drama goin' on," Ted said to Hal, who was shoveling fries down his throat.

Leon grew defensive. "Hold up… I don't have any drama goin' on. Last I checked, you're the only person I've seen dookin' it out in the parking lot, Mr. Young and the Restless."

Hal spit fries all over the table, making them jump back.

"Come on, man!"

Ted brushed crewed up potatoes bits off his uniform. "Am I the only one? Word around town is that you turned Hustle and Flow on a bitch in the unit."

Hal laughed and rapped. "Slap that trick! Whoop that trick!"

Leon tried to respond but Ted cut him off.

"What happened?" he asked. "Got mad because you couldn't turn a stripper into a housewife?"

At that exact movement, Adam walked into the OM. "Hey you guys," he called out, heading towards their table.

No one heard him.

"Man, she's just a piece of ass I hit," Leon said dismissively. "I went to tell her it was off and she got all emotional on me."

Adam was all ears. "Who are you guys talking about?"

Erin entered in the middle of the conversation, choosing to go straight to the counter.

Leon looked at the rookie, who was eager to know the ins and outs of being a correctional officer. "We were talking about Alexis, Erin's BFF," he said nodding towards Erin.

Turning from the counter Erin looked to see why her name was in their conversation. "What about me and Alexis?" She was already informed about Leon's unprofessional antics in the unit and wasn't really feeling him.

"Not you," Ted clarified. "He was explaining to us how his pimp juice went drier than the Mojave Desert."

Adam was confused. "What's wrong with Alexis? What did she do for you to be so disrespectful to her?" His lanky frame seemed to straighten just from the thought of them talking about her like that.

"Disrespectful?" Leon laughed. "Man, when you've seen one crazy broad you've seen 'em all. Me? I've been around the block enough to recognize a jump-off when I see one. And she's definitely one."

Erin couldn't stand for him to talk about her friend like that. "You're really actin' like a dick, you know it Taylor? Sounds to me like you're just jealous she dissed you the way she did."

"Jealous?" he laughed. "Some of these cells have tighter walls than she does. I'll never be jealous behind some cesspool escort pussy."

Both Hal and Ted's demeanor had changed. To them, Leon had crossed the line from joking to serious.

Adam was offended. "Now you need to shut the hell up. That's just rude!"

Leon stood. "Boy, who the fuck you think you're talking to?"

"He's right, Taylor," came Erin.

Adam wouldn't back down. "I'm talking to you, you fuckin' asshole."

Reaching out Leon, poked the frail bird chest of the youngster with each word he spoke. "It would be best if you watched your mouth when you speak to me."

Hal jumped up and got between them. "Come on y'all, let this shit go."

For a good five seconds, Leon and Adam stood there eyeing each other down. Then finally Ted got up as well, suggesting the three friends get back to work.

"He's not worth it Leon," he said. "And plus, break time is over."

Leon's ice cold stare broke and a smile spread across his face. "You know what? You're right."

Erin stood there with Adam as the officers left the OM. Once they were gone, she turned to Adam and said, "I know you're new here, but don't let that childish shit get to you."

He shook his head. "Nah, that ain't right that he's sayin' things like that about her. Alexis is a nice girl."

She agreed. "But you still can't let what other people say get to you like that. If you do then they win."

Adam nodded. "I know. You're right."

She smiled and said, "You like her, huh?"

For a second, he looked to blush, turning shy. Then he smiled also. "Yeah, a little."

Erin knew he did and she planned to tell Alexis all about it once she made it back to her post.

The day had drawn late with the sun setting far off in the West. Nothing unusual occurred other than the unforgiving sun rays. It was hot as hell and working compound for Ted was grueling. Making his way into the east corridor, Ted now looked to get inside. He'd just closed an activity's move so he had another hour to relax.

There she was.

"Hey you...."

Nurse Frost gave a slight smile. "Hey, I was looking for you."

Ted locked the door. He glanced down the corridor, seeing as a few inmates entered the Chapel. "Is everything alright?"

She exhaled a sigh. "Actually no, I miss you. Have you been thinking about what I told you?"

167

He wanted to wait before he let her in on his plan. Ted didn't wish to talk about it anymore. "Yeah, I've thought about it." He looked deep into her eyes. "I got this."

She didn't respond.

Not really wanting to be seen just standing, Ted said, "So why were you looking for me? I'm beginning to understand you more and more."

The shifting back and forth had given her away. Nurse Frost smoothed the palms of her hands on her scrubs with a mixture of fear and uncertainty, she said in a weak voice, "Ted... I'm-I'm pregnant."

Everything went silent. He didn't know what to say. All he could see was her pretty face and curvaceous body. How her hips and thighs looked in her uniform. Ted could see something in her that her husband couldn't and that was a future filled with happiness.

His silence startled her. Tears began to form in her eyes.

He smiled. "It's mine?"

She smiled and nodded.

"Well then, just be patient. I know what you want and you know what I want. That's for us to be together. For right now, let's keep this our little secret," he reached out and touched her hand. "Trust me, I'll take care of him."

A sense of relief came over her face. "I'm just ready to move on."

"I know. And you will." He looked up the hallway. "Listen, I gotta work a double tonight. How about you get that room in Blythe and I'll meet you around midnight?"

"Okay."

The evening came swiftly like every day in prison. After the 4 o'clock stand up count, the inmates were let out of their cells. Big Jake came out and set his chair out by the TVs. When he saw Ted was working his unit, he figured to approach the cop. The last thing he expected was to be approached.

"Calhoun!" Ted called out to him.

Dingo came out his cell and placed his chair next to Jake's. "Is he calling you?"

"Yeah, I'll be right back."

Asian Lee and a few of his guys were standing on the top tier. Big Jake looked at the little guy, every part of him wanted to extort the man.

Making his way to the office, Jake found Ted sitting at his desk. "What's up?" he asked from the doorway.

"What are you into? Meth? Weed? Heroine? Powder?" Ted asked straightforward.

Jake was a little stunned. "Drugs? Why, who's askin'?"

"Well, I gotta problem. If that offer still stands, I need it taken care of."

Being this conversation had taken a turn, Big Jake lowered his voice and looked around. A few guys were at the microwave and more were close at the phones. "Are you fuckin' kidding right now?"

Teds face held serious. "Do I look like I'm fuckin' kidding right now?"

"Okay, you talk and we'll see what it's gonna cost."

As Ted began to unfold his wish to have Lieutenant Frost mortally injured, Big Jake listened. He was flattered how the officer applauded his skill of brutality for the crime he committed, that's why he chose him. Jake would make it a point to emphasize that while he may not deliver the blow the job would get done.

Ted didn't give a damn who did it. Just knowing that vengeance would finally be served was enough for him.

Elsewhere in the prison…

The strobing bright light shone angel white, blaring in his blurry eyes. It was almost too much to look at. As Champ struggled to regain consciousness, the feeling of a tethered strap bit deeply into his wrists. His mind then registered the ones at his ankles, bracing them together. He was mounted against a wall with his arms stretched out, like a crucifixion.

Where the fuck am I?

As he processed the room, Champ saw a holding cell like none he'd ever seen. It was padded like a mental institution, all white with a plexiglass window that covered the cell wall with a small doorway. His eyes adjusted and that's when he saw someone in the cell across from him was looking at him. Champ looked and saw the corners of cells to the right and left of the cell.

"Arrrggg," he growled wrestling at the straps. They were too tight and he got no leeway.

The man in the cell was looking at him with blank eyes. He was just like him, in a white paper thin shirt cover. Champ sensed the man had been drugged like him.

Again, he struggled with his restraints. "Arrrggg…"

That's when the voice invaded the cell. "Inmate, do not struggle. It won't do you any good."

"Who's that? Get me out of here!"

No response.

The sound of keys could be heard along with the click clack of high heeled shoes. Champ was breathing heavily. There was something inside of him burning deeply. When he saw the black female doctor standing in front of his cell's window, he stopped panting.

She pushed a button located outside the cell door. It opened.

"What the fuck y'all got me in here for?" he asked.

That's when he noticed the syringe in her hand.

"What'chu got that…" he began before she took advantage of his inability to move. "Ahh!"

Sticking the needle deep into his arm, the lady doctor shot Champ up with a siren that calmed him instantly. Although he wanted to struggle, he couldn't. All he could do was look into the pretty brown eyes of the woman. Her chocolate face was stern with cold eyes.

Then he went out.

THE WALL

EPISODE 6
PLAYING WITH FIRE

1

With Leon out of the way, Adam went all out. He was determined to get Alexis if it was the last thing he did. All he needed was a little inside help from Erin. He needed her to put the good word in for him, which was what Erin did her best to do.

Alexis laughed. "That scrawny ass little white boy? What am I supposed to do with him?"

"I think it's cute he likes you," Erin said nicely.

"But why me?"

"Hmph… all that ass I'm guessing."

Alexis shouldered her backpack and give a slutty grin. "And your guess may be correct."

The night was finally over and both girls were headed home. This was the part they loved, yet craved, and that was the life of a correctional officer.

For days, Dino and Maniak discussed whether or not to take Gordo up on his offer. Once they decided to look into it further, Maniak spent time scoping out every facet of the job he knew so well. That very next delivery came to the kitchen and he was on it. From the driver's usual exit of the cab to talk to Mr. Casey, to the way they did the job under minimal supervision.

"I wish I could be there," Dino said as they discussed it outside.

"Maybe you can." Maniak had a great idea. "One time I got Bone to help me out when Fats got sick. All we gotta do is get you in the kitchen."

"Do you think you can get me in there?"

He nodded. "Yep. I'll get you in there ASAP."

"Alright then, I'ma holler at Gordo," Dino said confidently. "If his ass wanna get on the next train up out of here then we'll give it to him."

"Yeah," came Maniak, dapping his partner. "Fo' that bread he got that all day."

In B-Unit...

Today was going to be the day Joe-Joe made his move. He'd been plotting on how he was going to invest the cash money he brought from Coleman. Now he had his lick. He knew Alexis would bring the pack to him. All he needed to do was approach her with the proposition.

So putting the cardboard sign over the door's window slit, Joe-Joe grabbed the roll of tissue, and sat on the toilet. Wrapping his hand with a thick wad of tissue paper, he sat forward, placing his hand underneath his asshole.

He pushed.

Plop... out dropped one of the two latex gloves he stored. Round as a quarter and three and a half inches long, he wrapped it in the tissue and placed it in the sink.

Then he pushed again.

"Unnhh..."

Plop... squish... another dropped with a little company.

"Ah shit," he said at the sight and smell of the turd. The granola mix cleaned him out good.

Picking the second roll out, Joe-Joe wiped his ass and got up. Moving quickly, he washed off the gloves before drying them off. Then he sat at his desk and took the double wraps off each roll.

"Okay... there you go."

Each roll held twenty-five $100 bills totaling $5,000 in cash. The green backs were held tightly in the compacted roll. Joe-Joe reached in his locker and sprinkled both with baby powder, then he blew them off before putting small black rubber bands around them.

Taking time, he cleaned up. Once he removed the cardboard, he saw the dude they called Dino. Joe-Joe knew the man was on but he didn't agree with the prices. He wanted to get his own thing going.

In A-Unit...

Jake was headed to the shower. Taking his good ole time, he strolled, checking out the scene in the unit. Dingo was in front of the TV, Asian Lee was sitting and watching Sports Center, checking out the scores from the game and the officer working the unit was in the office just like he hoped.

It was shortly after 2 p.m. so there were only two showers being used. He hopped in the one that would give him a complete view so he could see everything when it went down.

With his headphones on, Dingo listened to the morning news with keen interest. Another terrorist attack on U.S. soil had the nation on alert. As he sat there, he looked over at Lee. The man was heavily involved with issues relating to his ticket. Since being in the unit, Dingo saw what Jake was talking about and how Lee thought he was better than everybody. He only cared about his own and helping the blacks.

He looked up at Big Jake getting in the shower and nodded.

Grabbing the remote control off the table, Dingo got up and went over to the Asian and Islanders' TV, and without any warning he changed it. The four guys sitting there looked at him like he was crazy.

"Hey man!"

He shrugged. "I just wanna check something out."

"Well do it on the Whiteboys' TV," Lee said.

"No, I'll do it where I want. You rice patty eatin' motherfucker!"

Lee was sitting down so when Dingo said this he froze, not sure how to respond. "Hey man, you gotta..."

Dingo wasted no time talking. Now the issue behind the TV got everyone looking. Tossing the remote, he lunged at Lee, throwing closed fists and striking the man hard. Two blows caught him across the head and face, toppling him over. The other Asians and Islanders jumped out of their seats to assist their shot caller.

"Get off him!"

A few Whiteboys were seated, actually ready for the scripted scuffle. So once the others went to join the action, they pounced immediately.

Dingo was on top of Asian Lee, pummeling him with blows. Jake was in the shower stall watching it all, so was the other inmates. Blacks were congregated to the side as was the Mexican gangs and Paisas.

The C.O. came out his office. "Break it up!" he yelled, stopping short of the melee.

Now, a full fight broke out with chairs flying everywhere. The officer hit the deuces…

Fight in A-Unit… all available staff… there is a confirmed altercation in A-Unit. Officer needs assistance…

The call from control came over the radio, sending Lieutenant Frost into response mode. He jumped up from his desk in the Lieutinant's office and ran out the door. Several officers standing around flanked him.

"Let's move it guys!" he called out.

Through the window, he could see other officers responding, running from different locations on the compound. Once he made it out the corridor, he took off sprinting down the sidewalk.

"Inmates on the ground! This is not a warning… get down now or you may be shot," the automotive recording announced from the tower. The gunman working stood in plain view with an AR-15 assault rifle in his hands. With dark Oakley glasses on his face, he looked like the Terminator waiting patiently to exterminate.

Digging his Hi-Tek boots into the concrete, Lieutenant Frost struck out, running like a sprinter to the finish line.

Meanwhile, lying in wait…

Chris and Jason loved a challenge. Just because they were locked up didn't mean shit. With Lucky, the three of them prided themselves on their ability to master the art of murder. When Jake informed them of the job request to kill not only an officer, but also a lieutenant, they looked at it as an opportunity to strike back at the people who sentenced them to all the time they were serving.

Call it justice.

Lucky saw it as a stepping stone. If they could accomplish this and get away they felt the officer working with Jake, could assist them in their own mission to escape. So seeing multiple advantages, they agreed. Plus, they never turned down a good paying job.

When the officers came running up the sidewalk, both brothers peeked from around the corner near the staircase next to A-Unit's entrance. This little ducked off spot leading into the unit was a blind spot, one of the few places where there was no camera mounted.

"Here they come," Chris told his brother. His blood boiled at the excitement.

With his hand tightly clutching the 8 inch ice pick, Jason gave a slight grin. He looked at Lucky who was kneeling down a few feet away from them. "As soon as Lucky creates the distraction, we move."

His brother nodded.

In full sprint...

Frost was in the middle of the pack of officers. Some were making it through the fence on B-Yard, darting to A-Unit. He knew time was of the essence because if weapons were involved then that meant a life could be lost. As soon as they made it to the end of the sidewalk, a white inmate jumped up and began running towards two Asian inmates with a knife in his hand.

Frost pointed. "Get him!"

He didn't know what this was all about or who was involved. There were a good number of inmates on the yard so he knew to keep his eyes on them all.

The officers tackled the white attackers to the ground as Frost and the rest made it to the A-Unit's slider. Already open, he made up the rear as the rest filed in through the sally port.

Crunched behind a concrete beam, both Jason and Chris pounced on the LT, who didn't see them coming. The two lunged pointy icepick blasts that plunged deep into his neck.

"Arrrggg," he cried out grabbing his neck. Blood gushed between his fingertips as he twirled to face his attackers.

Moving stealthily, the two brothers were like ghosts. Deadly accurate with their weapons, they now fled before the other officers could turn around and see them.

"Lieutenant!" one called out as he rushed to assist his wounded superior.

The wound burned as Frost fell to his knee, dizzy and becoming weak by the minute. Blood continued to pour.

"I need medical!" another officer called into his radio. "Officer down... the LT has been hit! Somebody call an ambulance."

While some officers rushed into the unit, others stood around their Lieutenant shocked and paralyzed by what just happened. Not one of them ever conscious enough to seek the attackers.

In B-Unit...

As Joe-Joe looked at Alexis holding the two rolls of bills, he measured her reaction. He didn't know how she'd respond, but it was too late now. He made his move as they both stood in his cell alone.

"I can't believe you got all this money," she said still staring.

"Look," he began. "Today's your lucky day baby girl. You've been blessed to be fuckin' with a real nigga. I see you're a go getter. Yeah, you got a good job. It's not because of the medical insurance and benefits they got for you. Trust me."

As he popped his game, she just looked at him. "How you know I ain't gonna get your ass locked up for this," she replied waving the bills at him.

"Because if you wanted to bust me for introduction you would've done it already."

His statement froze her, and they stood there facing each other. Alexis couldn't believe this dude. He was bold and the

177

look in his eyes said he was serious as shit. Exhaling a deep breath, she asked, "What exactly am I supposed to do for this? What do you want me to bring you? A phone? Drugs?"

Joe-Joe stopped her. "Here," he said handing her a piece of paper with a number on it. "This is my brother's number. Call him and he'll tell you everything."

Alexis looked down at the number and when she looked up, he had taken a step closer. She was now looking up at him.

"Just breathe," he said calmly. "If you just trust me, I'll make you a hundred grand in less than a year. You can leave these lame ass suckas you fuckin' wit around here alone completely."

Right when she was about to respond she heard the alert come over her radio.

"All unit officers... lock down your units... now! This is an institutional lockdown... I repeat, this is an institutional lockdown."

Alexis jumped as if she was scared.

Joe-Joe reached out and grabbed her by the shoulders. "Relax," he said in a soothing voice. "Lock down the unit. Remember, you got a job. But don't tell this to nobody, and call my brother when you get home."

Something in his voice moved her in a way she'd never been. She nodded. "Okay."

Then she turned and exited his cell. Smiling to himself, Joe-Joe rubbed his palms together.

Yeah, I still got it.

The emergency to save Lieutenant Frosts life was eminent as officers rushed everywhere...

Warden Maddox heard the call come over the radio when he was looking over some paper work sent to him from Washington, DC. He'd been so busy preparing for the upcoming visit from BOP's officials that he almost lost track of time. Now rushing down the corridor, he made it just in time to see the local paramedics as they wheeled his LT on the gurney.

"Move! Move! Move!" one of the EMT's barked as they raced.

Captain McDaniels met Maddox and filled him in. "Damn… he took a bad shot. He's bleeding like a pig."

The three EMT's made it to the barred gate, waiting for control to pop it.

"Get that gate open!" Maddox yelled to an officer already on his radio.

"He's convulsing!"

Lieutenant Frost's body jumped and thrashed on top of the gurney, legs kicking hyperactively.

Maddox made it to his side and saw all the blood. A paramedic was pressing a thick soaked gauze into his neck, trying to slow down the bleeding.

"No!"

The scream vibrated through the hallway drawing everyone's attention as Nurse Frost came running in their direction. Her face was torn in fear.

Maddox caught her, wrapping his arms around her body. Her face pressed into his chest. "Let them do their job. He'll be alright."

She shook her head. "Oh my god… oh my god," she cried peeking at the sight of all the blood.

Even though he tried to be positive, Maddox knew that the LT making it was slim to none.

2

The news of Lieutenant Richard Frost's death left the whole staff at USP Death Valley stunned. With the flag flying at half mast and the institution on lockdown, every officer and official there became that much more aware of the dangers of their jobs. The warden held a conference and addressed each of his personnel on the importance of security. This was the second officer that had went down since he arrived.

Now, as he paced in his captain's office, he couldn't believe the information he was being given. "Not one image of the attacker?"

Captain McDaniels shook his head regrettably. "The location was out of sight from any camera angle we have. For some reason, when the surveillance system was installed we missed the stairwells to the units."

"One hundred cameras on a state of the art maximum facility and not one in front of the units." Maddox couldn't believe his ears.

Two knocks came to the door.

"Come in," the captain yelled.

When Adam was called to the captain's office, at first he didn't know what to think. He opened the door and stepped in. "You called for me?"

McDaniels nodded. "Yes, come... have a seat."

Warden Maddox stepped over and shook his hand. "My condolences go out to you and your mother. Your father was a good man."

Adam took a seat. "Thank you."

"So," the captain began. "We know this is hard on you, and we thank you for continuing with work."

"I just wanted to come in," he said. "I figured there was no need in sitting at home when I could be helping to find who did this."

The warden and the captain shared glances.

"That's why you're going to go far working for the Bureau," McDaniels pointed out.

"So," came the warden. "You say you may have some footage from one of your drones that may help?"

"Yeah."

"Can you show us?"

Adam borrowed the computer at the captain's desk to go into the file of his drone flying over the top of each building, studying the ventilation system.

"As you see," he began to show them as they looked over his shoulder at the computer's screen. "I was just finishing A-Unit when the deuces went off for the fight."

The two ranking officers saw the train of staff responding with Frost in the middle of the pack.

"There he goes," Maddox pointed.

Adam continued. "Once they get almost to the building this inmate comes off a knee and threatens to attack these two men here."

They followed his finger.

"Next, officers respond to that while the rest continue."

"Do you think that was a distraction?" McDaniels asked.

"Could've been. Because look, as you see the rest go out of sight, here is when the attack must've came that killed my step pops." Adam slowed down the footage. "Watch closely and you'll see a brief glimpse of two white inmates emerging from that blind spot."

The drone's camera gave the overhead image clipped off by the building's ledge. The brief footage of the two men could clearly be seen. The top of their heads visible for only several seconds.

Warden Maddox was pleased. "I want that image blown up. We need to find those two. Whoever they are, they know something."

The captain agreed.

"And you," the warden addressed Adam, "Good job."

"No problem, that's what I'm here for."

Meanwhile…

Ted stood in Nurse Frost's office in medical. Many of the PA's and doctors were tending to other duties, such as delivering prescriptions to the inmates in their cells. The two lovers had been keeping their distance since the murder. Now for the first time they met to discuss what their next plans were.

"So no one has questioned you?" she asked him.

"Nope. Being how I was off when it went down, I don't see why they would."

Rubbing her puffy eyes, Nurse Frost sighed. Ever since she returned to work she'd been stressed. "IA and FBI must've asked me a million questions, and I'm just tired."

"Well," he began. "Internal Affairs is gonna do that. It's protocol, so don't get yourself all in a bunch behind it. They don't have any leads at all. How 'bout your lawyer? What's she talking about?"

"You mean the life insurance policy?"

"Yeah."

She shrugged. "She's on it. I guess she'll notify me when its ready."

Ted moved a few loose strands from her forehead. "Listen," he said in a comforting voice. "It's all over now. You don't have to worry about him anymore."

She smiled. "I know. It's just…" she shook her head. "I can't believe he's dead."

The two of them were silent.

Nurse Frost looked up at him. "Can I ask you a question?"

"Yeah babe, whatever?"

"Those guys… the ones who you got to kill him…"

"What about them?"

"Did you promise them anything?"

Ted picked up his Jansport backpack and tossed it over his shoulder. "Like I said, it's over. Don't trouble your pretty head. I took care of it, that's all you gotta know."

She just smiled. "Okay."

After promising to see her later, Ted left medical and made his way out onto the compound. Like usual, the day was a scorcher. With the place being on lockdown it was almost peaceful walking the compound. It reminded him of when there was less inmate population. He looked up at the gun tower and thought back to the day Rosalez opened fire. There was something about the prison that brought the worst out of them.

Once he made it to A-Unit, Ted relieved the officer working that post and settled into the office. After he was in there for about twenty minutes, the buzzer to the front slider rang out, signaling the delivery of the inmate's meals. He got up to go retrieve the cart and found Hal there making the drop.

"They got'chu on kitchen duty?"

"Yep," came Hal. "A little O.T."

He nodded. "Yeah, me too. This lockdown got us all puttin' in a little extra work."

"Well, I need it. I plan to use it for my upcoming trip to Hawaii."

Ted laughed. "Surf the waves?"

"Surf?" Hal looked horrified. "Hell naw! Man, them sharks been eatin' people alive."

"That's for sure." Ted grabbed the cart filled with paper sack lunches. "Well, let me get this shit passed out. That way the rest of my night will be smooth sailing."

"Alright," Hal replied. "Maybe I'll stop back by later on."

"Yeah, do that."

Out of 264 bunks in the unit, there was a count of 226. Once he made sure he had enough bags, Ted began the task of passing them out. It had been a while since he had to do it but he didn't mind. He knew it was best to go on and get it out of the way.

Up in Big Jakes cell…

The man stood in the window watching Ted making his rounds. For days he had been wondering if Ted was going to work his unit again during the lockdown. Jake had done everything he was asked. Even sacrificed his brothers in the process. Dingo was in the hole, as well as Asian Lee. Lucky was gone too but he'd gotten word that Jason and Chris got away.

Just like he planned.

Jake was so glad he didn't have a cellie, that way he could ask Ted about his payment. After waiting patiently at the window the officer finally made it to his door. "So, what do you think?"

Ted looked at him and without saying a word; he opened the latch on the door. Then he grabbed a bag off the cart and shoved it into the cell before slamming the latch hard.

Wham!

The bag fell on the floor at Jake's feet. For a moment, he just stood there in disbelief. Ted had moved on to the next cell. Some black guys were begging for an extra bag but all Jake could think about was the stone cold look in the officer's eyes.

Did this motherfucker play me?

Reaching down, Big Jake picked up his sack lunch and turned from the door. Right when he was about to toss it on the counter, he opened it.

"Well, hello Dolly," he said smiling.

Inside was airtight compressed blocks of weed, tobacco and a few white blocks of cocaine and meth. There were also a few lighters, syringes, and a small glass pipe. Big Jake estimated the total amount of product to be in the tens of thousands.

Tap... Tap...

He looked up at the door and saw Ted looking through the window smiling.

"Oh, that's just for starters," the man assured him.

He nodded. "Anytime brother. Anytime."

The Internal Affairs investigation, in conjunction with the FBI, lasted a full three weeks. Keeping the institution on lockdown, the warden and captain continued to look into the images they were working with. Although they had one in the SHU, they weren't able to identify the assailant responsible for Lieutenant Frost's death.

By the fourth week, the decision was made to bring the institution up to partial status. The inmates were unlocked, but only regulated to their units. No outdoor recreation. Food services was brought to full operation so kitchen workers were called to prepare the meals to give nourishment to all those weakened by the lockdown.

When Dino went to breakfast, he saw an assortment of food; hot oatmeal, pancakes, eggs, a fried mystery meat patty, an orange, butter, and milk. The place was packed with everyone from his unit, which is how the administration was feeding. He filed through the long line, grabbed a tray and made it to the serving counter. Maniak was standing behind the line with Bone. Both were in their kitchen attire.

"Boy you look like you starvin'!" Maniak joked.

Dino shook his head. "Four weeks! They caught me slippin' too. I only had one jar of peanut butter, eight Mackerels, and a few bags of chips."

"No soups or rice?" came Bone.

He waved him off. "You know I keep a bunch of soups and shit…"

Maniak cut him off and said to Bone, "That fool lying. He got big shit up there."

Dino gave him a serious look. "Nah, for real! You know I don't eat a lot of stuff. Granola and shit. I had just filled out my commissary list."

Maniak pulled closer to the counter. "I spoke with Mr. Casey."

All during lockdown, Dino was eager to get back on their mission. "What did he say?"

At that moment, the double doors behind the counter busted open. The food administrator, Mr. Casey, exited barking orders.

"Maniak… Bone…" he called out using their nicknames, which he did to everyone. "It's a mad house back here. We're gonna run short if we don't get some more oatmeal cooked and eggs fried."

Dino could see things were busy. A cook was at the open fryer behind the line, cooking eggs.

Mr. Casey continued as Bone and Maniak stepped through the door. "Patterson, Maniak said you're try'nah work in the kitchen," he said to him out of nowhere.

He shrugged. "Yeah, you got a spot for me?"

"When can you start?"

Dino dropped the tray. "I can start now if you need me to."

Mr. Casey nodded his head. "Eat first. At least that'll get you out of the unit. You can hang out up here with us."

Everybody knew it was cool to work for the man. He was the type to make a lot of food just because he knew the inmates were hungry. He had a lot of compassion, yet he still did his job.

Hearing this, Dino got his food and knocked it down real quick. He was chewing, swallowing, and drinking in the same cycle. When he looked up, Maniak was standing behind the line, beckoning him to hurry up so he cut it short.

"I needed that," he said making his way behind the line.

"That's right," came Maniak following. "Now you can see what we're working with. Plus, you're not gonna believe this."

"What?"

Maniak smiled. "We gotta unload today. I'ma try to get you on the truck with me."

Dino couldn't believe his luck. Fresh off a lockdown and he got the opportunity to execute things almost immediately. This was almost the perfect story. All he needed now was to figure out how to execute.

For three hours, he attended to minimal duties like help cook, clean pots, and help Bone carry bags from the warehouse. It was there he saw the layout as Bone explained his process to retrieve the shipment. They were coming from back there when he saw Maniak and Fats accompanying Mr. Casey.

"Super Bowl?" Mr. Casey was livid as he spoke to Fats. "The *Ain'ts* will never win another Super Bowl. Everybody know the league gave y'all the one in o-six because of the hurricane."

"Gave it to us?" Fats said in shock. "Man, we took dat. When was the last Super Bowl y'all got?"

Dino heard about their vicious debates from Maniak, who was playing the sideline and loving the action. "What's up y'all?"

Mr. Casey was about to respond to Fats comment but instead asked Dino, "Who's your team?"

He shrugged. "I don't have one."

"Well do you watch football?"

"Yeah."

"Who's better? The Cowboys or the Saints?"

Both Mr. Casey and Fats stood there looking at him like his answer would settle a well battled trial that lasted for weeks. Maniak's eyebrows raised and Dino took the side that mattered most. "I think the Cowboys are a better team. Although he's old, Tony Romo still got it."

Fats tossed his head back and grabbed his forehead. "Ahh-naw…"

Mr. Casey laughed. "Everybody knows it. Matter of fact… Fats you're fired!"

"Fired!" the man cried.

"Yeah, for the week. That costs you a week's worth of hustling my sugar. Instead, come on Dino."

Maniak was thoroughly intrigued while Fats shook his head. "Okay… okay… I got'cho, ass," he said laughing at his boss.

The man just waved him off. "Come on y'all, let's go unload this truck."

Dino laughed at the small crew. He knew Mr. Casey would never replace Fats with him permanently. This was their way of getting some laughs in on each other. Little did the man know, if it was up to him they would be the one with the last laugh.

3

"**D**amn nigga!" Petey Moe cried. "You always wanna stay in the unit. Come out!"

To everyone's surprise, they called a recreation move after the 4 p.m. count. The rumor was they'd stay on semi lock down until the end of the week, but it seemed that the warden had other ideas. Joe-Joe was glad because he saw Ms. Green arrive to work to see if she brought his package or not.

"Look," he told Petey Moe. "Yo ass ain't gon' do nothin' but try to slide next door and fuck wit' your little play thang." He knew his homeboy had already began his sexual exploits with the homosexual.

Smiling Petey Moe said, "I ain't gon' lie, slim. Shawty got that good good. If they would've let her move up here with me, I'd be in the unit all day too."

Joe-Joe cared less for all the details. "Just tell the homies I said I'll catch 'em when they let us back up. I'm on somethin'."

"A'ight."

Laying back on his bunk, Joe-Joe continued reading the Phat Puffs Magazine he subscribed to. He liked it because it kept some of the most exotic chicks in the urban community on display. Each one thick and fine how he liked them. He figured he'd wait until the move closed, letting everyone go outside, before he got at Ms. Green. He called his brother earlier so he knew she took care of business. The only thing left to see was if she brought his stuff in or not.

Meanwhile, out in the yard...

The game was called Omaha. Five cards in your hand, but only two played. With five also on the board each poker player tried to make the best hand, betting as each card on the board was revealed. Jinx ran his poker game with an iron fist, rain, sleet, or snow. Fresh off lockdown, he brought out the blankets, cards and chips, knowing his players would be ready to go.

"Bet a hundred," came a Mexican dude named Flaco.

Blue looked at his hand. The board flopped a diamond flush 7, 5, 9. He was sitting on the K and a three. "I got second best. You better have the ace. I call," he said tossing the chips into the put.

Flaco smiled.

"Cards comin'," Jinx called out as he flipped the turn card. "Ace of diamond."

Blue started smiling. "Ah shit! I caught one fakin'!"

Flaco shook his head. "Check."

"Oh hell naw! Ain't no checkin' now!" Grabbing his chips, Blue started counting the piles he had before him. "Three-hundred and eighty dollars. I'm all in."

Flaco's smile now turned to a sly grin. "I call."

Jinx turned the river card, a 4 of clubs. Blue tossed his K and three of diamonds on the board. Flaco tossed the six and eight of the same suit.

"Ah shit, he had the straight flush," Jinx said.

Flaco clapped his hands in excitement. "That's right! Come to daddy!"

The pot was almost $1,000.

"Fuck!" Blue said frustrated, then he got up from the table.

After Jinx finished sorting out and taking the houses cut, he called Butta from Virginia to fill in. "I'll be right back. Let me holla at this nigga."

Blue had made it over to his homeboys. Bone, Tray and a few more Crips were standing against the fence line. They were listening to their homeboy, Meech, from Long Beach 20's explain why he whooped and ran up his cellie during lockdown.

"This mutha'fucka was try'nah play wit' his dick while I was sleep," Meech explained. "Cuz, I woke up because I heard some rustling and shit."

"Wha'chu do?" Bone said laughing.

"At first I just laid there, listening. Then I heard some squishing sounds. So I jumped up and this nigga was on the top bunk with his legs all cocked pen, wackin' his shit. On Long Beach Twenty Crip, I snatched that nigga off the top bunk and beat his ass. That bitch ass nigga hit the button ASAP."

Tray said, "I'm just glad you ain't go to the SHU behind that nigga."

"Yeah," came Bone. "That's why I don't cell up with them weird ass niggas. If it ain't no homie, I ain't fuckin' with it."

"What's up Cuz?"

The group saw Blue and each shook his hand with the ritual Crip shake.

Bone nodded in the direction of Jinx. "I think ole boy from DC lookin' for you."

Blue turned just as Jinx made it to them. "What's up?"

Jinx removed his paper, which had the amounts of everyone's wins and losses at the table. "Look, you down two g's. How do you wanna handle this?"

Blue twisted his face up. "Damn nigga, we just came off lockdown!" Then he waved the man off. "I'll get you when I get you."

"What!" Jinx immediately went to reach for the knife at his waist.

However, Tray and Meech were quicker on the draw. Both men pulled stainless ice picks from their pockets.

"Hold up," came Bone stepping in between them.

Inside B-Unit...

When Joe-Joe saw her coming up the stairs, he went back to his cell. There wasn't many inmates in the unit so he planned on getting an update from her. By the time he turned around, she was opening his door, stepping in.

"Hey..."

The sound of her voice was sweet, but full of panic. "Hey," he answered. "So you hollered at my people?"

With darting eyes, Alexis looked out the cell window, then back to him. "Yeah." She laughed. "Boy, I can't believe you got me doin' this."

Joe-Joe stood there and watched as she unfastened the button of her slacks. Then unzipping them he saw the cotton white panties she wore.

She smiled. "A bitch had to tuck that shit real good."

He nodded.

Sliding a hand into her panties, Alexis probed between her thighs and removed a tightly compressed package, flat and thin. She handed it to him. "Hold up," she said now shoving her hand down her backside.

Joe-Joe inspected the pack in his hand and despite it being heavily wrapped in tape and plastic, he knew it was heroin.

"Here you go," she said handing him another. "I know that's two ounces of kush."

"How you know that?"

The question paused her. There was no more sign of panic. "Listen, I ain't bringin' nothin' in here without knowing exactly what I'm carrying. That might've been a bomb or somethin'."

The sight of her standing there like that, with her pants still unbuttoned in the front, did something to him. He looked down and saw the smooth brown skin of her lower stomach and pelvic area. A whisk of hairs lined her panties. When he looked up, she was looking at him. "Baby girl I wouldn't have you do that."

Alexis began to straighten herself out, grinning at how she turned him on. She saw the rise of his dick print in his sweat shorts. "I got two more that I'll bring when I feel comfortable."

Feeling like he had the upper hand, Joe-Joe jumped out there and risked his luck. In one swift movement, he stepped forward. "Hey…"

She looked up at him as he leaned in and kissed her lips. No part of her body resisted him as he wrapped his hands around her waist, sliding them down her hips and ass.

Joe-Joe was lost in the softness of her body pressing against him. He looked down and saw she closed her eyes. He knew he was her type, a real thug-type street dude. So he over powered her attempts at playing tough.

She broke the embrace. Fear was back on her face. "What are you doing? Why did you..."

He laughed. "Relax." He looked past her and out the doors window. "Nobody's in the unit, so when you step out, do it casually. Go down the tier and hit another room." Then he stared her down to make sure she understood.

She nodded. "Okay, I'm cool."

With lust in his eyes, Joe-Joe looked her up and down. "Nah... baby, you better than cool. You wit' me now."

At first, she seemed unsure but then she smiled. When she closed the door, Joe-Joe stood there looking at the first of many packages to come. How things unfolded for him thus far had him rethinking his relocation to the West Coast.

"Yeah," he said to himself. The 30 grams of heroin and 2 ounces of kush motivating him. "It's on now."

Back on the yard...

Petey Moe was talking to Alicia. Ever since the homosexual touched the compound, he had been right next to him. Everybody knew not to fuck with him or they'd have to answer to Petey Moe. The two were inseparable and already been sexually active.

"Damn baby, my counselor doesn't wanna move you over there."

Alicia sat with his hands between his thighs. "And my counselor doesn't want anyone in my cell either. What do you think we should do?"

Petey Moe had been in Alicia's unit many times. He even fell asleep in his cell after their first encounter. "Right now, let's just wait. Until I can get'chu over there. I'm not gonna accept a cellie."

Alicia pouted his lips. "Me either."

With his face twisted up Petey Moe said, "I know you better not."

That's when he saw Jinx in a confrontation, making him get up and head in that direction.

On at Jinx…

Bone looked at Tray. "Put that up Cuz."

Tray put his knife back in his pocket so did Meech.

Turning to Blue, Bone gave the man a stern look. "Cuz, you owe the table two racks?"

With frustration on his face, Blue looked at Jinx and then Bone. "Yeah, but this nigga actin' like we ain't just come off lockdown."

Jinx looked like he wanted to sock Blue right in the jaw. Before he could turn this into an all-out war, Bone said to him, "Man chill out. I got this."

Petey Moe stepped next to his homeboy. "What's up?"

"This nigga owe the table," he said. "And I need mine, slim."

Bone looked at Jinx. "Aye, let me holler at my homeboy a sec'. We'll get to the bottom of it," he said.

Petey Moe and Jinx stepped aside. Once they were out of earshot, Jinx filled his homeboy in.

"Aye Moe, I was finna'h blast that nigga on the spot."

Petey Moe was agitated. "If these Crip niggas don't handle this shit… we ain't givin' a fuck about bein' in Cali. We'll shut this whole yard down."

Bone looked at Blue. "Alright," he said, looking at his watch. "You got by tomorrow to have that. If not, on Fo-Tray I'ma DP you myself."

The mentioning of getting disciplined was enough. He knew in his case a DP consisted of knives or getting beat with master locks. "Cuz, I just couldn't get in touch with my girl."

As soon as he got a good understanding with Blue, Bone made his way over to Jinx. "Look, don't let that nigga back on the table. Give me your info, and I'll shoot you the money myself."

Despite still being upset, Jinx agreed. "Alright, that's cool."

Bone noticed how the man kept mean mugging both Tray and Meech. "Also, if you got a problem with my other homeboys... I mean, you tried to reach for your shit," he said shrugging his shoulders.

Jinx waved it off. "Nah, don't trip."

When Bone walked off, Petey Moe looked at his homeboy. He was confused. "Why would you have a problem with them other niggas?" Petey Moe asked.

Still looking their way, his eyes connected on both the Crips, who pulled their weapons on him. "It ain't nothin'. They just exposed their hand, that's all."

Over on A-Yard...

Big Jake handed the netted laundry bag to Jason like it didn't have tobacco, crystal meth, and cocaine in it. Despite the fact that the compound was filled with people, the transaction went unnoticed.

"Let's find a table," came Chris.

Ever since the two brothers executed the life of Lieutenant Frost, they remained cool during lockdown. It went so smoothly that they couldn't believe it themselves.

Finding an empty table, the three men sat.

"I was told Lucky only got a knife shot," Jake informed them. "When he gets out I'll give him his cut. From here forward I'll give each of you a percentage of everything that comes in."

It sounded like music to their ears. Jason wanted to make one thing clear. "Just remember we'll need him to bring in a phone and possibly a gun." Jake's face cringed at the mentioning of a gun.

Jason saw it. "Now, we talked about it."

"Okay, let's just get him comfortable making his moves. I know y'all want to get out of here. But it may take some time."

Chris interjected for the sake of his brother. "Well, time we have. Just as long as you make it clear to him," he said in a serious tone. "Because just like his officer buddy... he can get it too."

THE WALL

Across the yard...

With Asian Lee being gone, Dino had a lot of loose ends to
tend to. Once he returned from the kitchen, he shot outside to
speak to the Asians. From what they explained, his partner was
in the SHU behind fighting over the television. To him
it sounded insane. They were sure he'd be back soon.

Bouncing around, Dino then spoke with Donnie, who was
out collecting money owed to them. They both agreed to speak
more once they got back in the unit. Dino's real reason
for hanging out was Gordo so once he saw the Mexican,
he immediately made his way towards the fence to greet him.

"Aye... Dino!" Gordo was smiling. A group of his
Paisas was with him.

"What's the word?" Dino asked, smiling himself.
"You tell me. You're the man." Separating himself from his
brothers, Gordo stepped to the fence line.

"I may have some good news."

"I knew I could count on you," the Mexican said. "So
let's hear it."

Dino told him how he was allowed one week to work in
the kitchen, particularly in the position that would allow them
an opportunity to attempt the escape. "The way I have my shit
comin' in is where I'm at. I got a chance to see every step
myself. And to be honest, I can see it working."

Gordo listened to every word Dino said, excited to hear
the improvements. "Using the phone you sold me," he began. "I
was able to pull map information onto the screen, which helped
me to see a route through the desert I can take."

"A route through Death Valley?" The idea seemed
ludicrous. "How do you plan to travel all the way to Mexico
through the desert without dying of heat exhaustion? It gets
hella hot out there."

Gordo laughed. "Since I was a boy, I've traveled in and
out of the United States, carrying backpacks and bundles of
cocaine and weed for the Cartel. It's how I got my start. There
are numerous trails and underground tunnels between our
countries."

"But you'll need water."

The man shrugged his shoulders. "The trip will be difficult, yes. It's a price I'm willing to pay. Plus, I still have strong ties to the Cartel. Even though I have been replaced, I'll contact some close associates to arrange a convoy to pick me up. But first things first, I need to get out."

Dino nodded. "Well, the next delivery will be in seven days. In the meantime, I'ma get all the details in order."

"When you do, let me know," Gordo replied. "I'll make sure you receive every dollar I offered, that way if things don't go as planned... you'll see my appreciation."

In medical...

It had been days since Ted last spoke to Nurse Frost. Ted wanted to see how she'd been doing, and if she'd been questioned anymore.

A female dentist came out of the double doors leading towards the practitioner assistant's rooms, looking at a clipboard.

"Is Nurse Frost back there?"

She nodded. "Yeah, she just got back."

He smiled. "Thank you."

Making his way to the back, Ted searched the hall until he saw her come out of one of the rooms. "Hey there," he called out.

Hearing his voice, Nurse Frost seemed alarmed. She turned and in a surprising move she said, "Uh... Listen, I'm a little busy right now. So could you..."

Ted sort of jogged a few steps towards her then stopped. "I just wanted to check up on you."

A look of fear and suspicion grew on her face as she looked up at the camera sitting above them. "Yeah, uhm... I'm good. Just a little behind on my work, that's all."

He went to touch her shoulder but she jumped. "What's the matter with you?"

Her eyes were on the camera again. With tight lips she just said, "Listen, I think we need to keep our distance for a while."

The suggestion hurt Ted, taking the wind from his lungs. "But…"

Without letting him finish, Nurse Frost quickly turned and marched in the opposite direction. She left him standing there, wondering what in the hell did he do wrong.

In the SIS office…

Adam was sitting in front of the computer looking over the images from his drone when he saw something peculiar. An image blotched on top of the heads of the two unknown white or Hispanic men who appeared from the stairwell caught his eye.

"What in the hell is that?"

Using the mouse, he enlarged the picture until it filled almost the whole screen. Squinting his eyes, he saw whatever it was; both men had the exact blotched mark. Then it hit him.

"They're tattoos."

He leaned back in his chair. He knew the last piece to he and his mother's plan was now coming together. Perfectly.

THE WALL

EPISODE 7
PUSHING PAWNS

1

The morning sun rose in the sky, casting rays of light through the cell's window. Jason and his brother managed to become cellies for the first time since catching their case. It was welcoming to be able to do so, considering the life sentences they were serving. Now, wrestled from their slumber, both brothers stirred in their bunks knowing their unlock was approaching.

Chris stretched and yawned. After Big Jake gave them a cut of the drugs he got in, the brothers took the liberty of smoking two fat joints and multiple cigarettes. The effects had them both groggy and slow.

Pop!

The loud metallic sound startled both of them, making them lurch up to look at the door. In a *woof!*! It snatched open and in crammed a fleet of correctional officers.

"Get down! Get down!"

"Face down!"

Jason was on the bottom bunk. No sooner than he tossed the covers off his body, several officers grabbed him. "What the fuck…"

"Get Down!"

Chris snaked his hand underneath his mattress and grabbed the ziplock bag with the drugs. "Okay…okay," he said tucking it in his gym shorts quickly. He then tossed both hands in the air.

Captain McDaniels stepped in barking orders. "Get him down and cuffed!" Jason was now on his stomach in the small space getting cuffed up.

"Cap, what's this all about?' He got no answer as the tactical unit abstracted them from the cell.

In B-Unit...

Joe-Joe didn't know why it was taking so long to unlock, but he wasn't tripping on it. This only gave him more time to separate and bag up his product. After Alexis dropped the kush on him, he immediately got with Petey Moe. They were finally in a position to make some money and he needed all his homeboys on deck and ready to hit the compound hustling. So he told Petey Moe to be ready in the morning to issue out the kush.

Sitting at his desk, Joe-Joe made small packages of $100 chap stick-cap measured bags of weed. In total, he got 146 out of 2 ounces. That would total $14, 600. He wanted to wait on bagging up the heroin until he found a reliable client. His goal was to sell three hundred dollar grams, or possibly all of it for a reasonable price.

The smell of the exotic kush reeked. Mixing a concoction of prayer oil and water into a nasal spray bottle, he sprayed the cell. Then, washing his hands he freshened up. His plan was to give each of his homeboys at least five caps to sale. He'd charge them seventy-five dollars, letting them keep twenty-five.

It was after 8 o'clock when the doors finally began to rack. Jumping up from his bunk, he looked out and saw they were coming out. He saw Petey Moe, who came out his cell and looked up at his.

The officer working their unit was a quiet black dude, young, and very respectful. When he opened Joe-Joe's door he spoke and kept it moving, unlocking the doors. Petey Moe came up the stairs and followed him inside the cell.

"Damn," his homeboy said smiling. "So baby made it happen, huh?"

He nodded. "Yeah, like I said when we got here we're gonna lay the foundation for when other homies come."

Smiling, Petey Moe said, "She gotta fat ass too. A nigga would love to get some of that."

"Man, stay on business." Joe-Joe knew his freaky homeboy got sidetracked easily. "Plus, she can't stand you."

Joe-Joe pulled the large plastic bag filled with the caps of kush out his pocket. Outlining his intentions, he explained his plan to hit the compound with the product. Petey Moe would be the one who hit the others with their issues. Once they turned in what they owed they could get more. Anyone who made the mistake of messing the money up would be dealt with.

Simple as that.

Back in the SHU….

The Special Housing Unit ran an early morning recreation move around 5:30. From tier to tier, on each range, an officer would call to see who wanted to go out. Many refused, preferring to stay in their cells. For Skull and Snake, it was a must they got out to get some fresh air and to exercise.

The Rec Yard for SHU inmates consisted of 15 cages big enough to hold up to twenty people. It was a procedure to only allow ten at a time. Whenever Skull and Snake went out, the officers would keep them separated from everybody else; today they had company.

"So," Lucky began. "They got me for a knife only. Hopefully I'll be out of here soon." Listening as Lucky told them of everything that went down on the yard had the two men's attention. Since he arrived in the SHU, both Skull and Snake were trying to get him in the cage with them. Now that he was, they got the whole rundown.

Snake laughed. "Ole Jake finally made a move on Lee." He shook his head. "I can't believe it."

"Well I can," came Skull. His comment held a bit of disdain and emotion.

Lucky caught it and asked, "Why did you say it like that?"

Shrugging, Skull replied. "He couldn't stand him anyway. Jake is the type of person who would move a person out the way if things aren't going how he wants. But fuck that, I'm wondering why he hasn't tried to send nothing back here to us." Since being in the SHU, Skull couldn't stop mentioning to Snake how he felt Jake used them. Snake could sense his partner felt Jake maybe did the same to Lucky and his boys. The whole time the three men spoke the SHU officers continued to bring others to the cages.

At the far end of the row, Skull saw someone who looked familiar. He tapped Snake.

"Hey, isn't that Critter familiar?"

Snake looked through the mesh fencing and made out the little white boy they hadn't seen since the night they punished Biker Dan. "Well if it isn't that rat son of a bitch. Hey you little fuck!" he called out. "You know you're dead right?"

The sound of his voice caused Critter to look up in fear. Shuffling around in a cage, all by himself, he still looked spooked. "Oh...hey, man. Aye look, I haven't said anything. Not one word," he called back. They knew better. That's why he was separated by himself.

"Who's he?" Lucky asked.

"He's the fucker who was in the room when we gave it to the Whiteboy we were telling you about," Skull replied. "They're using him as a witness to prosecute us."

"You lying shit. You better hope you never land foot on another yard where we got brothers. If you do, you're dead," Snake called back.

An officer escorting a black dude into a cage, with a few of his people stopped in front of their cage. He looked at Lucky. "Aye, I got a message for you."

"For me?" he asked with a look of surprise.

"Yeah, it's from your Irish brothers. We just brought them back here. They said watch who you talk to."

Hearing this, Lucky quickly took note of the officer's nametag. It read Tisdale. "Fuck," he replied disappointed. "Thanks."

Skull and Snake overheard it. "Well," came Skull. "Two more fell behind some shit Big Jake initiated. Why is it that everybody falls but him?"

The question caused all three men to ponder the answer themselves.

In Administration...

Alexis walked into work with Erin at her side. The two met in the parking lot and their conversation got so intense they carried it into their job. In hush tones and whispers, Erin chided

Alexis about what she revealed concerning the extra money she was making. With a family rooted in corrections, she felt that Alexis was making a grave mistake. "I just don't wanna see you get into any trouble."

"I'm not," Alexis assured her.

Erin wasn't convinced. "My cousin used to do that shit. For a long time he got away with it. But the guy he used to bring shit in for turned on him."

"Turned? How?"

Erin stopped there in the hallway and faced her friend. "He set him up….called the FBI with the same cell phone my cousin brought him for a thousand dollars. My cousin was caught with some cocaine and heroin. They gave him fifteen years."

The information seemed to put Alexis at a pause. "Damn, that's fucked up."

"Yeah, that's why I'm telling you. Five thousand dollars isn't worth your freedom. You gotta good job now." Erin started walking again. "Just think about it."

As they passed the door to the Officer Mess Hall, it opened and out stepped Adam. When he saw Alexis he couldn't keep from smiling. Erin thought it was cute.

"Hey Erin," he said. "Hey Alexis."

"Hey Adam…"

Alexis saw how he was looking at her. "What you doin, Adam?"

Shuffling his feet, he dropped his eyes. "Ah, nothin'. I just needed some salt packets."

Trying to strike a conversation, Erin said, "So Adam, we just heard you might've found the inmate who murdered your dad."

"Step dad," he corrected. "But yeah," he continued with his chest poked out a little. "I was able to use digital images I retrieved from my drones' camera to identify them. They had four leaf clovers on top of their heads."

Hearing him sound so proud made Alexis want to flirt so she reached out and touched his arm. "Oh Adam, that sounds so brave of you. To think, you might've solved the whole case before the FBI could."

Now he was skinning and grinning. "Well…Yeah, I guess I did."

"They should just go ahead and hire you to SIS full time," Erin suggested.

"They have. Warden Maddox and Captain McDaniels put me in full control over outer and inner compound security. I control every camera angle and perimeter visual for the whole facility."

Both girls looked impressed.

Adam turned to Alexis and said, "I know you're on your way to work but I wanted to ask….can I take you to dinner some time?"

Alexis' eyebrows rose. "Dinner?"

"Yeah. You know, just for fun." Never before had she seen him this bold.

Smiling at Erin, she looked back to him and winked. "Sure, Adam. Sure, I'll go do dinner with you."

The acceptance left the young man elated as they continued on to their paths.

In A-Unit….

With Asian Lee out of the way, Big Jake turned into "the man." The other Asians were not equipped to retaliate with the Whites being that there were so few. To help matters, Jake spoke to them assuring that Dingo wouldn't return, and the issue behind the TV was uncalled for. From there, he proceeded to put himself into a position that would enable him to take over the gambling also. He had a plan to open up his own ticket now.

After going to the yard, Big Jake spoke with Eddie from Utah. He and Eddie were cool and there was mutual respect between them. When Jake handled the issue with Biker Dan owing him, Eddie appreciated the backing. Jake knew Eddie was in for dealing meth in Salt Lake City, so he planned on recruiting the man on the team.

"I swore off sellin again," Eddie told him as they sat on the bleachers. "After the FEDS took all I got…..shits been rough on me."

Big Jake understood. "Well, now you got a chance to make it right. They took it from you, now you get it back from them. Right off the same prison they're holding you in."

"You know you're right. Count me in," Eddie thought hard on it and said.

And just like that Big Jake had convinced yet another person to participate in one of his grand schemes.

2

Nurse Frost's shift was over and all she wanted to do was get back home. She exited the administration's building and walked towards the parking lot. All she kept thinking about was her lawyers persisting advice to staying low and cooperating. Until all of the issues pertaining to the Bureau's investigation was over, she was to stay tight lipped.

As soon as she made it to her 2020 Toyota Tacoma, a figure rounded the SUV she parked next to. She jumped in nervousness.

"Calm down," Ted said. His eyes were puffy from nights of unrest.

"Why are you jumping out from behind cars?" Nurse Frost gave him an angry look.

Ted stood firm. "Because I can't catch you otherwise. I need to talk to you."

"About what?"

"Us!" The tone in his voice made her eyes look to see if anyone was around. When she did, she saw Leon at his truck, talking to the little spanish girl, Erin.

"Lower your voice," she told him. "Somebody might hear you."

Ted stepped forward, pinning her to the SUV. They were sort of hidden between cars at an angle. "Who cares if anyone hears me. I don't know why you're so nervous. You didn't do shit."

"I know I didn't," she replied sternly.

"Then what's wrong?" Grabbing her around the waist, Ted stepped into her body. "What I did, I did for us." Wiggling from under him Nurse Frost pushed Ted slightly.

"I think we need to end this."

"End this?"

"Yeah," she said. "Just for a minute. Until things blow over."

Ted was mad and confused. "But what about you? The pregnancy?"

Fumbling, she managed to get her keys out and opened her truck's door. " Look, let me say thanks for everything. Right now let me get my head in a right space. It is not you, it's me."

As she got inside her truck, Ted stood there dumbfounded. By the time she pulled out her space and left the lot, he was still standing in the same spot. Inside he felt like a complete fool, lost in a love triangle.

Across the parking lot…

What Erin didn't tell Alexis was how Leon had started flirting heavily with her. Almost every day he managed to find a way to bump into her, spitting his best game. It was their last run in that really caught her attention. An incident involving her bending over and him commenting on how delicious she looked. Erin saw a hunger in his eyes; like she looked like a sweet cherry pie that attracted him. It had been a long time since she was made to feel like this.

Now as she stood next to her car, Erin looked into Leon's eyes as he did his best to seduce her.

"Just one taste," he said begging. "I promise, I'll be gentle." His creep request to lick her pussy showed a freaky side she found amusing.

"Leon, we're at work. That would not be proper."

He tugged at the front of her pants. "We're not at work until we clock in," he tempted.

Gently, she grabbed his fingers as they played against her pelvic area. Biting her bottom lip she replied. "Not this time."

"Maybe next time?" He smiled.

"Maybe," she nodded.

Inside B-Unit…

Once the activities move was called, inmates rushed outside. A variety of events were transpiring. The 4th of July was quickly approaching and like every year, the prison made different things available to the population. There was a host of recently released movies, outdoor events and competitions that would span over the course of that weekend. The main attraction for the evening was a three on three basketball game and team handball.

Joe-Joe got things moving. He had his homeboys moving caps of weed left and right. His mission was to stack the money he gave to Ms. Green first. He went about everything with caution, choosing to hold off on moving the heroin until he found someone reliable to buy it.

When he first saw her come into work, he wondered if she brought in his second package. After she finished the recreation move, she gave him a look that told him to go to his cell. So getting up from in front of the TV, Joe-Joe walked up the steps and waited in his cell, faking a look back, he saw no one paid him any attention. The only two people in the unit watching TV were so into their shows that he was sure they were safe.

He was changing his shirt when the door opened. Alexis came in and saw his naked chest and began to smile.

"What?" he said choosing not to put on the t-shirt in his hand.

She shook the look off her face. "Nothing, you just ….your body looks really good."

Joe-Joe thanked her as she began to go about her routine of removing the package she brought in. Unbuttoning her pants, Alexis proceeded to dig in her panties. As she did, he looked into her eyes and smiled. Once she removed the final plastic bundle and handed it to him, he took the liberty to step closer towards her.

"Hold up," he said before she could button up.

Alexis was feeling the lust between them. To say she expected him to kiss her again would be a lie. As soon as he began, she lost all sense of reality and responsibility. She chose to fall into the risk of the moment, overcome by her own lust.

Feeling her soft body, Joe-Joe's dick jumped iron-hard like steel in his shorts as their tongues touched. The smell of her perfume was intoxicating. His hands groped down her pants as he felt the cotton of her panties.

She pulled away. "No, we can't…."

He stopped her. "Just trust me." Moving past her, Joe-Joe reached next to the stainless steel toilet and picked up a cardboard window cover he made, and placed it on the door. Then he turned and faced her; standing there in his cell staring at his body like a kid in a candy store.

"What are you doing to me?" she asked.

"Only what you want me to do."

Knowing time was of the essence, Joe-Joe made his move. In the years he been down, he'd never had a chance to have sex. So there was no wonder why he was so aggressive with his hands. With the precision of a master, his fingers fumbled across her uniform's shirt buttons, plucking them open. The dark blue bra she wore held plump breasts tucked in the lace designed cups. Filling his hands with both, he kissed her deeply. She moaned into his lips, her hands caressed his bare chest. Leaving them to trail down his stomach, Alexis couldn't help but to glide inside his shorts where she found an ever growing surprise.

Joe-Joe broke their embrace. "Turn around," he told her, his hands were inside her panties, feeling her wetness.

Doing as she was told, Alexis let him lead her towards the back of the cell by his desk. There she placed her hands on the table while he began peeling her work slacks down her fat ass. When he saw how her panties were nudged inside her moist crack, and how they plopped out of it turned him on even more.

"Damn," he said.

She thought about what she was doing and the idea turned her on even more. The excitement of it, plus knowing how big his dick was made her want to feel it inside her. Arching her back, she looked over her shoulders at him. "If you gon' do it, do it. Show me what you got."

Her aggressive advances made Joe-Joe grit his teeth. Pulling his long dick out, he stood behind her, guiding its fat circumcised head between her legs. The heat from her pussy breathed on him as he found her center.

"Ssss...."Alexis cooed as she felt his girth stretching her opening. She was wet so it made him entering easy. His rough hands tightly gripped her hips as he sunk deeper.

The heat from her pussy was like heaven. As he penetrated, Joe-Joe never imagined her being so soft and wet. Her insides seemed to be extra juicy. Gripped by the feeling, he pulled back and thrust into her deeper. His dick slamming into her so hard her ass cheeks and thighs jiggled. Hitting her without a condom wasn't a thought.

"Uhn!" she cried, biting down on her lip. Joe-Joe was lost in lust as he repeated the drill. All the years of built up sexual deprivation created an animal out of him that took over.

Wham! He slammed his dick deep into her.

"Uhn!" Alexis cried out. Her face contracted in ecstasy.

Wham!

"Oooh....shit," she squealed into the crux of her arm. She tried to mask how good his hard cock felt.

Crunching into a good position, Joe-Joe used the ab training work and strength in his legs to continue giving Alexis a dick down she could only dream of. As he looked down, he saw pussy juice running down her legs and completely covering his rod. Using one hand, he dug into her shoulder to give him more leverage. Now he was riding her with the rhythm of a horse.

Meanwhile...

Adam was feeling like the man. Even with all the drama surrounding his step-father's death and his mother's promiscuous behavior, he was finding purpose in life. Warden Maddox and Captain McDaniels asked him to submit any security related upgrades he felt would help the prison be more secure. Them believing in him and with his new interest in Alexis blossoming, things couldn't be better. All he could think of was taking her out on a dinner date. There was something about her that turned him on. Maybe it was her big fat ass.

As his mind drifted, Adam continued his aerial tour of the eastern wall of the prison. He marveled at the height of *The Wall*. A prisoner scaling it was impossible. Even if they could, the desert would run them back almost immediately. Maneuvering the control, he flew the drone inches from the bricks only to elevate overtop the back of B-Unit. He saw an officer walking across the roof top and smiled.

"Soon you may be out of a job, buddy," he said from the comfortable confines of his new office. The officer waved, recognizing the new "Wiz-Kid" running the show. The drone whizzed yard side and Adam saw all the inmates on the yard. The place was way over 1,000 in population and it looked as if all were out. Like usual, his drone was a ghost in broad daylight. None of them seemed to look up as he descended slightly against the units' buildings.

"Spider-Man…Spider-Man. Does whatever a spider can," he sang, directing the craft so that its belly crawled on the bricks.

Angling the two cameras forward, Adam continued to descend across cell windows. As he passed them, he got a glimpse inside the rooms, invading the privacy of each one. He saw a group of four smoking, some guys cooking, reading, working out and other things. But as soon as he crossed the next, he had to pause, unable to believe his eyes.

"What the fuck?" he said in a low voice. His heart sinking by the minute. On the other side of the glass he saw his dream girl, Alexis, getting fucked from the back by a black dude with dreadlocks. In a knee jerk reaction, he jammed the joystick, sending the drone looping out and crashing back against the building.

"SHIT!!" he screamed as the monitor went to static.

Inside Joe-Joe's cell…

His shorts were now at his ankles. Rocking steadily, Joe-Joe's nuts swung like a pendulum as he continued ramming Alexis' ever so wet pussy. He knew she came by how much she moaned moments prior. Now she pushed her ass back, begging him to finish.

211

"Cum for me," she said.

The feeling of cum boiling deep down in his loins begin to stir. With one hand at the small of her back and the other cupped around her thigh, he plunged deeper.

"Fuck!" he growled as he shot his load. His dick jerked and jumped as cum fired into her wetness. Joe-Joe's strong legs began to buckle a little as he savored the feeling.

That's when they heard two taps at the door.

Knock...Knock.

"Yo..."

When the door flew open, Joe-Joe snatched his dick out of Alexis in time to see Petey Moe step into the room. "Aye Moe," he began.

His homeboy's face was of pure surprise as he saw Alexis exposed. She tried to straighten herself. "Oh, uhm, excuse me."

But moving quickly, Petey Moe stepped closer. "Nah, my bad, slim," he said to Joe-Joe. "Am I interrupting something?" Seeing her naked turned him aggressive. "Damn baby."

She tried to move past him, but he pinned her in the corner of the cell.

"Hold up," he said pulling his dick out.

Joe-Joe tried to intervene. "Not like this, Moe."

But Petey Moe had his mind made up. "Shit, y'all both know I ain't missin' out on this."

Alexis froze in fear as she contemplated the situation she was in. She regretted ever doing this. For a moment she thought Joe-Joe was going to speak up for her but he chose not to. So right there, for the next 10 minutes, she endured the most degrading experience of her life. She let Petey Moe abusively rape her body, ending with sodomy. When it was all over she was left in the cell to clean up the bloody mess. Never had she imagined this would be the outcome, not for $5,000.

3

Word spread around the compound that it was the whites who had Lieutenant Frost killed. Dino didn't find it a coincidence how all of a sudden Big Jake had a dope sack. Maniak also informed him that the DC cats were pushing caps of Grade-A chronic, as if they had a Cali plug. But despite all this Dino kept his eyes focused on his task with Gordo.

Like promised, Mr. Casey kept him on for a full week. During this time, Dino and Maniak cased out each step of their plan to help Gordo escape. Maniak explained the details of how to get Gordo into the back of the kitchen and to a hiding spot for waiting. Then when the time was right they would sneak him to the back dock while they distracted the supervisor. From there, Gordo was to get in the back of the U-Haul styled delivery truck. From what Dino saw inside the truck, when he helped to unload the last time, it carried enough for a person to hide. It provided all the right cover.

The morning of the attempt Dino woke up and called his daughter. Needing someone on the streets he could trust, he was having her get the $100,000 from Gordo's people. Once she indeed confirmed the money was in a bank account, Dino then went to get ready for work. When breakfast was called he shot out the unit in search for Maniak.

"So he sent it?"

Dino nodded. "Yep. All we gotta do now is get him on that truck. After that, he's on his own."

Feeling good about their come up, the two men headed into work. Walking amongst the others going to breakfast, they braced themselves to do the impossible.

In C-Unit...

The whole reason for him wanting a cell phone was for this. Gordo spent every other moment learning more and more how to utilize all the benefits for it. If he wasn't handling a matter in the prison concerning his people, he was in his cell getting lessons on using it from the youngsters. They showed him how to access the Internet, view sites, maps, and find contacts he needed to aide in his escape.

Now, with the moment at hand, Gordo exited his unit like he had every morning. Usually he was accompanied by his right hand bodyguard person but after assuring his Paisa brother he needed to go and speak with someone privately, he headed to the kitchen. He told no one his intentions. The only ones who knew were the two helping him and the Cartel.

As soon as he entered into the kitchen, he saw his Paisa brothers sitting at their assigned table. They seemed happy and festive as usual. Always recognizing him when he arrived, he waved back at a few looking his way.

"Buenos Dias," he called out. Making his way through the line, he saw Dino standing at a side door that led to the back. Once he got near, it opened up.

"Come on," came Dino.

Gordo stepped out of the line and did as he was told. It was not out of the ordinary because inmate workers arrived to work all the time through that door. So as he entered the kitchen, he stepped lightly across the fleshy mopped floor, trying not to slip. "The supervisor is in the office. Follow me."

Dino led him through the kitchen and when they got by the office, he saw the two staff working. One was the boss and the other a C.O. Gordo slid past the window undetected, following Dino. A couple Paisas saw him but kept moving.

"In here," came Maniak, pointing to a storage room next to the door to the warehouse.

Gordo went inside.

"You'll wait here," Dino said. "The truck should be here soon. Until then just be as quiet as you can."

Dino already explained the plan. He was to wait in the room and once he got the signal he'd come out. From there he would be led onto a truck, where he'd hide amongst pallets piled with 50 pound bags and boxes.

"Will you be okay?" Dino asked.

"Yes, I'll be fine. Just go," he said, closing the door. The storage room was filled with seasonings. With the light off, he scurried into a dark corner and waited patiently. Silently he said a prayer to Santa Maria.

Meanwhile...

Dino and Maniak returned to their task of looking busy. With the morning kitchen crew finishing the meal, the two headed to the office to check on Mr. Casey.

"I'm glad you're here," the man said to Maniak when they walked up. "I need you to grab that list you compiled of all the damaged boxes we received from the deliverer. Our distributor said they're gonna replace these items."

"Alright, I'll go get that now."

Dino followed as Maniak went to the small locker area assigned to those with his type of job.

"I think the truck is on the way."

Dino looked at his G-Shock watch. "This early?"

Maniak smiled. "Yep. That's better for us."

After Maniak retrieved the paperwork the supervisor requested, him and Dino hung around waiting. Mr. Casey confirmed that the truck was coming so all that was left to do was be patient. They almost had a close call when one of the morning cooks went to the small storage room for some seasoning. They both swore he'd see Gordo. But he didn't, which meant the man was well hidden.

When the moment of truth arrived, Mr. Casey exited the office with his clipboard in hand. "You two ready?"

They nodded.

"Well, let's get this over with."

Coming in early...

When Alexis found out the officer working before her in B-Unit fell ill, she volunteered to come in and finish the shift. Since the incident with Petey Moe, she vowed to get him back.

She also wanted to check Joe-Joe. Neither one knew how upset she really was but she planned on showing them.

She was the wrong bitch to fuck with. When she walked in the unit, she found Hal covering. He was seated at the desk in the office looking like this was the last post on earth he wanted to work.

"I thought you'd never make it."

She forced a smile. "Well, I'm here," she said, sitting her backpack down. Alexis waited for him to get up and gather his things.

"Okay," he said. "I'll see you later."

The moment he walked out, the fire and anger inside her reignited. She saw a few inmates hanging out on the tier and in front of the televisions but she didn't look for anyone in particular.

"Excuse me, Miss Green."

The voice made her to look up. Standing there, Joe-Joe tried to appear humble. "Not right now," she said.

"Alright," he said. "But I just wanted to tell you I handled that."

Grinning, she gave him a serious look. "Oh, I don't need you to take care of nothing for me. I'm a grown woman. But thank you anyway."

As he left, she put her things away. She could see Petey Moe in the background, trying to read her, but she acted as if nothing was wrong.

Yeah I see you, she thought as she intentionally met eyes with him. *We'll see who has the last laugh.*

Back in the kitchen...

The back dock of the kitchen was enclosed by a fence that when deliveries came would be opened. Then the truck's flatbed or forklift would pull up to the dock's ledge where the items being delivered could be removed. For 45 minutes, Dino and Maniak unloaded bags of rice, oatmeal, Farina, beans, flour, and boxes of cereal to the warehouse. This was the heaviest day Dino ever had to work.

Now, as they stood on the dock listening to Mr. Casey argue with the truck driver, both men waited patiently for their chance to strike.

"My company is not responsible for those damaged items!" the driver barked. "I'm only the driver!"

Mr. Casey wasn't trying to hear it. "If you're the one damaging them, then you are responsible!"

The dock set high as the supervisor and the driver stood ground side. Maniak was standing with his fingers intertwined in the fence next to the rear sliding door of the truck. Still open, the loading area of the truck was partially filled with other large food items. Many of which the deliverer had to drop off at another location.

Dino had drifted back towards the door leading into the kitchen.

"Well what am I to do?" Mr. Casey asked, he was now all up in the driver's face.

"Hey, call Washington for all I fuckin' care!"

Maniak turned and waved for him to go. Dino did just that. Moving fast, he busted through the door and hustled down the short hall. Immediately, to his right was the storage door. The camera was mounted far off, on the back wall but he ignored it. He gave the door two quick taps.

Knock...Knock..

Then he turned around the corner. He heard the door open and out came Gordo.

"This way," he whispered.

The Mexican rounded the corner and the two rushed back towards the door. When Dino opened it, he heard the supervisor still in a heated debate.

"What's your name, pal!"

"Mr. Deez," the driver replied.

"Deez?"

"Yeah," he said with emphasis. "Deez nuts!"

Maniak waved them over. Moving fast, Dino led Gordo to the truck, then pointed inside. With a look of fear and confusion, the once top ranking official in the Sinaloa Cartel

217

seemed to have doubts. "Will this work? They'll inspect this at the gate."

"They don't inspect the vehicles delivering shit to the kitchen," Maniak lied.

"Come on, "Dino pressed. "We don't got time to worry now."

"You're right," Gordo snapped out of it. Then stepping into the back he found him another hiding spot.

Dino stepped in and saw him crouching behind some boxed. "Lay down and I'll place some more on top of you."

Gordo did just that. After a few boxes, he was soon covered neatly. Both Maniak and Dino stood back and admired their work.

"What do you think?" Maniak asked him.

He shrugged. "We're about to see."

Right on cue, Mr. Casey came up the steps. "Close it up you guys. Let's go."

The driver slammed his door with excessive force. *Wham!!*

Mr. Casey cursed. "Asshole."

Pulling the rear door down and locking the latches, Maniak and Dino went about their work like it was a normal day. Whether Gordo made it or not, they both were able to earn the money he offered, the rest was up to fate.

In B-Unit…

When the compound officers came in the unit, Petey Moe knew she called them. Now they were all up in his cell, shaking it down. He was mad as hell but if this was her way of standing up to him, he'd take it. To him, the brief piece of pussy he got was well worth it.

"Look at that slut bucket bitch."

Joe-Joe looked at Alexis as she switched her ass down the tier, checking guys and going in cells. "Slim, you jive raped the girl. What you expect her to do?"

He was still upset. "Fuck that bitch. As long as she keeps bringin' in that pack, I don't give two shits." The door to his cell opened. A tall crew-cut white boy in his early 30's stepped out. His 6'4" height held with extreme posture.

"Hey Mosely," he called to Petey Moe. "Come here for a sec." The two other officers exited the cell as well. One of them locked the door.

"Why y'all lockin' my cell?"

"Step over here," a short stocky black officer said.

Not wanting to draw any attention, Petey Moe did as he was ordered.

"What's up?"

The tall officer circled around him. "Put your hands behind your back."

"What's this…" he began to say.

The short officer and the extra one stood at his side, helping him cuff up.

"Who's cell phone was that?" the tall C.O. whispered. "Talk to me."

"What!" he yelled. "Nigga, I ain't got no cell phone!"

The cuff clenched extra tight on his wrists.

"Just relax."

Joe-Joe stood way off. He had all his dope tucked in his boxer briefs. A small crowd watched from various places. He saw Alexis dip off in another cell.

Petey Moe cursed protests in his defense. But no matter what he said, the officers weren't hearing it. They rushed him off to the SHU carrying a small iPhone in a plastic bag. Once they were gone, Joe-Joe simply returned to his cell. He didn't know the full story, and how his homeboy got the phone but something told him not to exclude Alexis.

The officers shack at the East Gate…

Ralph Payne was a 30 year vet in the Bureau of Prisons. Now, at 57 years old, he was looking forward to his last weeks on the job. When he was given the officers shack at the East Gate post, he saw it as a way to cruise. No unit fights, stabbings or drama; only laid back desk sitting and phone answering. Every now and then he'd have to check someone in or out. Either way, it was gravy.

219

When the delivery truck returned, Ralph found the driver mad as a cat in a pillowcase.

"I'll tell you, Payne," the man said jumping down from the cabin of the truck. "I can't wait to be in your shoes. I'm ready to retire."

Ralph laughed. "You'll be there soon. But what happen that has you red as a beet?"

The driver explained the altercation with the kitchen supervisor. As Ralph listened to the issue about damaged boxes and responsibility, he ran the mirrored stick underneath the truck. Then they walked around to the back where the driver opened the rear door.

"….and I told him 'Deez Nuts!!"

Ralph stopped and doubled over in laughter.

"Mr. Casey's a good guy, but you really got him with that one." Then stepping up from the rear bumper he entered the rear compartment.

"I just don't understand why he can't see I'm not the one responsible for that," the driver concluded. "You see, that's why I need to get my own truck. Do my own business with who I want."

Hearing this, Ralph stopped and faced the man. "That's a good idea. My brother-in-law just bought a used eighteen wheeler for thirty thousand. He's got jobs lined up and down Pacific Coast Highway."

Smiling, the driver agreed. "Thirty-Thousand? That's not bad."

Ralph jumped down. "I'm tellin' you. You'll be into the cash flow fast. Shit, you'll be retiring and relaxing in the sun with me in no time."

For a good five minutes, both men continued on with their conversation with dreams of sailing the coast of Spain. Their discussion was only interrupted when the phone in the shack rang.

"Well," the driver said looking at his watch. "I gotta get back. I'll see ya' next week Mr. Payne."

Ralph headed to the shack. "Alright. It'll be my last."

The driver closed the rear door and hopped in the cabin. While Ralph was on the phone confirming to Tower 3 the truck's departure, he flipped the switch, opening the gate. As it rolled wide the driver hit the horn twice.

THE WALL

EPISODE 8
JUST GETTING STARTED

1

The C-Unit officer whose count was off by a person called it in. After several attempts at not being able to locate the inmate, the yard was recalled and everyone was sent back to their cells for count. When Warden Maddox was contacted on the matter, he was in the City of Palm Desert attending a conference at the College of the Desert. Leaving the issue to his AW's, he returned only to find them still unable to find the missing person.

Why did I ever take his job?

The thought crossed his mind a million times. Why he chose to transfer to the middle of nowhere was beyond him. Ever since he arrived at USP-DV there had been nothing but problems. He was beginning to think if it wasn't for bad luck he wouldn't have any luck at all.

It was well past 12 in the morning and no one was leaving. Maddox had his captain, two AW's, and his new lieutenant, Greg Anthony, in the conference room analyzing data. Anthony had just come from USP-Allenwood in Pennsylvania. At 40 years old he was a no nonsense black man with a reputation for being hard on inmates. They were all huddled around images of the inmate entering into the Mess Hall where he disappeared. Despite the searches, they now believed he may have actually escaped.

"Sir." Each man looked up and saw Adam standing in the doorway holding a file.

"Come in," Maddox said with a wave.

Adam entered. Loving the excitement and trying to impress his superiors he said to the warden, "Sir, I think I've found something you should look at. It's concerning our missing man."

"Okay, give it to me," Maddox said.

Making his way to the computer, sitting at the far end of the table Adam sat, and tapped a couple of keys. The warden and circled behind the young Wiz Kid as he pulled up camera images.

"Now," he began. "This is from today inside the kitchen. It's in a hallway, at the back."

Each of them watched as Adam fast forwarded to the time-frame of 9:45 a.m., then he slowed it back to normal speed.

"Here," he said pointing. "This is Jorge Suniga, our missing person, coming out of a storage room. As you see, he peeks his head out after another inmate knocks on the door. They're exiting, he rounds the corner out of sight."

"Where did they go?" Lieutenant Anthony asked. "What's down that other hallway?"

It was Captain McDaniels who responded.

"The back dock."

Maddox spoke loud and clear. "I want all those images freeze framed. I want every delivery made to the kitchen pulled. Call the local officials. We got one fugitive."

The command sent every man scrambling. In the center of it all, Maddox contemplated his situation more.

Damn, why in the fuck did I take this job? he asked himself again.

In B-Unit….at 2:15 a.m….not an insect moved. A light breeze entered, flowing along the unit's concrete floor…

Inside the cells, the central air conditioning made the small cubicles nice and comfortable. Dino tossed the blanket from his body and got up. For hours he stood at his door watching as compound officers counted and recounted every man in there. To say he wasn't a little paranoid would be a lie. It wasn't until midnight that he decided to lay down.

It worked.

He almost couldn't believe how easy it was to get Gordo out of there. For it to be a high security prison, the guards made it as easy as walking away from a halfway house.

Standing at the toilet, Dino relieved himself. Out of habit, he flushed the toilet as he pissed, masking the sound.

"Ahh," he yawned.

Pop!!

The metallic sound caused him to piss all over the back wall of the toilet as the cell door flew open.

In C-Unit…..at 2:15 a.m….dust balls rolled across the concreted floor like tumbleweeds on dry desert land...

Maniak laid on the bottom bunk with the covers tucked tightly over his head. His cellie, Twan, was balled up as well. The two were snoring loud and dead to the world.

Pop!!

"What the ….."

As soon as both men heard the clack of the doors lock, they sat up. Immediately, they saw a group of officers trying to open the door. The only problem was they had their emergency lock in place. It consisted of a thick french braided sheet connected to the bedpost, and hooked onto the cell door. The hook latched onto a tightly woven sheet wrapped into the doors breathing holes. The connection kept the door despite the officers pulling it.

"Open the door, Now!!" an officer barked

Maniak hopped up. This was what he feared. He put the lock in place for moments like this.

"Aww Blawd!!" Twan yelled as he jumped down from the top bunk. Quickly, he began grabbing the stash of kush he had, jumping for the toilet.

"Open the door or we're smokin' you out!" came the next order.

As Twan began flushing, Maniak swallowed the emergency stash he had on stand-by. It consisted of six compact balls of kush in latex balloons. Doing the same, Twan managed to swallow his just as the flap on the cell door flew open.

Boom!!

The first canister exploded, sending smoke to fill the room. A thick cloud engulfed both men as they did their best to cover their eyes. Moving about the cell, they got rid of all the contraband just as the gas began to burn their eyes and lungs.

"Open up or I'm sending another!"

"Alright," Maniak barked. The pepper spray was too much. He had everything taken care of so he grabbed his makeshift lock and unhooked it.

"Move! Move!!"

Snatched from his hand, the cell door burst open quickly. The correctional officers rushed in and with extreme aggression, they grappled both Maniak and Twan, wrestling them from the cell and onto the ground.

"Aye Man!" Twan yelled. His slim physique bent like a pretzel at a ball park.

Maniak stayed quiet as the four officers pinned them to the ground. He knew exactly what they were there for. But for forty thousand, he didn't care. He knew the power of silence.

Inside the warden's office...

Maddox had been awake for an entire 22 hours, unable to catch a moment's rest. His night had been spent trying to locate the missing person. Local officials managed to find the delivery truck used in the escape 2 miles up the road on the interstate. The driver was killed, leading them to believe their fugitive had someone on the outside waiting on him.

As for his staff, Maddox instructed them to perform an all-out round-up on the individuals seen in the camera footage from the kitchen. With these men in the SHU, he now focused on another matter involving the ongoing investigation of his lieutenant's murder. With high-ranking officials flying in from Washington, he knew he needed to clean up some of this mess before he found himself without a job.

Fifty miles southeast of the prison.....

Death Valley's desert stretched to the Nevada border making for a difficult journey. The heat was almost unbearable at as early as 9 a.m. Traveling with no water, Gordo trekked through the dry and parched land driven by his will to return home to Mexico. With his iPhone, he used a map off an app to direct him to where he was trying to get to. His years of experience as a child smuggling drugs into the U.S. came back to him as he marched on. He'd already sent word and a convoy was being deployed by the Cartel to pick him up. All he needed to do was make it to the border.

After making it inside the delivery truck, Gordo stayed hidden, even when it was inspected by the guard working the gate. He was scared to death, praying to not be found. Thanks to a frivolous conversation and lazy security, he was able to escape. His opportunity to escape the confines of the truck came when the driver stopped at a gas station along Interstate 40. He knocked on the inside wall and it brought the driver to the rear door, curious to see what was causing the sound. What he found was Gordo as he leaped out, stabbing the man once in the jugular vein.

He dropped next to the pump, gasping for air as blood poured from his neck.

Grateful that no other vehicles were present, Gordo left the scene, dashing into the desert undetected. He knew it was only a matter of time before the clerk in the station came out and found the body. Probably even longer before the police arrived at the place since it was in the middle of nowhere so he used the time to put as much distance between him and the station.

He looked at the phone's screen and wiped the sweat from his forehead. Seventy more miles…..

In the SHU…

The area to process inmates came equipped with a central office called the Central Booth. Four officers worked the Special Housing Unit at a time, tending to the many things that needed to be done. Although the inmates were on 24 hour lockdown, the SHU could get very hectic; fights between cellies happened all the time.

Surrounding the Central Booth, in a half moon, around the left wall, were ten barred cell. For the past twelve hours, Dino sat in the cell they put him in, waiting for them to take him on a range. Maniak was in the cell next to him. The two of them was trying to get some information about why they were being held.

"Excuse me," Dino called to an officer he knew from working the hot trash crew.

"Yeah, what's up Peterson?"

"Have you heard anything?"

The officer shook his head. "To be honest with you, right now all types of shit is goin' down."

"Like what?" came Maniak.

The officer looked at them both and smiled. "Let's just say, if any of it has anything to do with you....it's not looking good."

2

The shower in the small cell was welcoming as Petey Moe let the hot sprays wash his body. With his cellie outside on the rec-call, he got some alone time. Being in the SHU could test your tolerance and his was running thin. There was nothing like being in a cell with someone all the time and his young homeboy, Weezy, was a pain in the ass. All he wanted to do was talk shit, and tell stories about "fucking bitches."

At the moment, he was being held under investigation and was served an incident report for the cell phone. Petey Moe knew they weren't going to let him back on the compound, so he awaited his fate. He didn't care either way. As long as he didn't get another charge for Ms. Green crying rape he felt like he got away with murder.

After about a good 20 minutes, he cut off the water and stepped out butt ass naked. He grabbed his towel off the bunk and was drying off when he heard the knock.

"Oh, excuse me."

Petey Moe saw the Asian man duck out of the cell's window slit to give him some privacy. He stood there dripping water with his dick hanging down to his knees. "Who's that?"

"Um…medical."

Wrapping the towel around his waist he went to the door. "Medical?"

The man's tag read Hong. Standing there with a clipboard in his hand, the clean cut man looked no older then twenty-five yet had a head full of gray. "Yes. Are you Peter Mosley?"

Hearing his government name made him tense up. "Yeah, what's the deal, doc?"

Mr. Hong referred to the clipboard that was in his hand. He flipped over several pages as he spoke. "I'm the lab technician and I'm here to inform you of a serious matter."

Not knowing what the lab technician was there for he said, "Serious matter, like what? What the fuck you want?"

The technician was not intimidated. "Are you familiar with a man named Andy Hill?"

"Andy who? I don't know no Andy."

Hong's finger traced the page on the clipboard. "Or also known as Yellow or Yella, Boo-Tang, Sunshine or Alicia Keys."

At first the names only made him mad but the last caught Petey Moe's ear. "Alicia Keys?"

"Yes, he is a fellow inmate of yours here at the facility," Hong looked at him as he spoke.

"Short cat, slim, with long hair and a little waist."

Uncomfortably the technician nodded. "Yes, I believe so."

"What about him?"

Like a professional, Hong laid it all on the line. "He's a transfer here from a medical facility. When we conducted our monthly review of his case, he informed us that you two engaged in sexual relations. Is that true?"

Now he was really upset. "Man, what the fuck are you all at my door askin' me about who I'm fuckin' for? Why? Is you gettin some of that ass too?"

Emphatically Hong replied, "No."

"Well then, why you askin' me?"

Clearing his throat the doctor continued. "For medical reasons."

Petey Moe was now confused. His eyebrows frowned up. "What type of reasons? What's wrong with that nigga?"

With an even tone Hong said, " He has HIV; something he's carried for many years now."

The three letters were like a shot from a 12 gauge in his ears. "He has what?"

"HIV. That's why he was sent here, Mr. Mosley. It was a discipline transfer. With this prison also listed as a medical treatment facility, we figured sending him here would help to monitor his infection."

As the technician spoke, all Petey Moe could think of was all the times he snuck to that unit and had sex not knowing the boy was infected. On the spot, it was as if he could feel a tingling in the head of his penis as his balls shriveled in their sacks.

"So," the technician asked again, snapping him out of his trance. "Have you had any sexual relations with him?"

Not knowing what else to do, Petey Moe exhaled a long sigh and lied. "Hell nah! Now get the fuck away from my door!!" Then he returned to his task of drying off.

In the Administration building…

The SIS offices were busy with officers, racing to find the missing inmate. Local officials and others were calling in every other minute with possible leads and sightings of a Hispanic man matching the description they sent out. Amongst all the chaos, Adam sat in his personal office space looking at the monitor. Since the escape, he wanted to fly his drone out into the desert to see what he could find. But with the warden needing the surveillance video he had no time. Well, now he did.

Glad that he upgraded the model to one that could travel up to 100 miles remotely, Adam navigated the craft above the desert land with faith. If he were to actually find this inmate he knew it would get him a promotion faster than anyone to ever work SIS. He knew it was a long shot because someone surviving the hot desert elements on foot for that long would be a hell of a task. He also searched for tire tracks, just in case an off road vehicle was used.

"Hey Adam," a coworker called out.

Taking one ear bug out he looked up. "Yeah."

"We're ordering pizza. You want something?"

"Yeah, two large pepperoni," he answered.

Not expecting any visitors, Adam saw his mom enter the building. After speaking to some of the officers, Nurse Frost made her way back to where he was.

"Well hello," he said mildly. His eyes still on the screen as he navigated the remote control.

"Hey," she replied. "Is that your plane you're watching?"

"Yeah, it's called a drone, Ma."

"Oh, okay. That's your drone picking up those images?" As she spoke she watched the monitor as desert land, cactuses, and rocks blanketed the earth.

"Yeah, I wanted to fly it out earlier and see if I could pick up any tracks from our fugitive."

She seemed impressed. "I think that's a good idea."

Still focused Adam asked, "How have you been? Are they still messin' with you?" On that last part he lowered his voice.

"No," she informed him. "My lawyers said it's out of our hands now. I don't have to worry about any more questions."

"Good," he said. "And the insurance money?"

She leaned down and kissed his forehead. "Soon honey, soon. The paperwork is all done. The only thing to do now is wait. Our plan will finally be complete. I just have one more thing to do."

Listening as his mother give him the update, Adam felt good about how everything turned out. Yeah, tragedy struck but it was for the best. Now him and his mother could finally live the life they deserved in peace.

In the parking lot...

Ted and Leon strolled from their cars carrying backpacks and water coolers. Now at the entrance to the administration building, a small group of news reporters stood next to their respective station vans. Cameramen angled their equipment, trying to capture images of the prison guards.

"It's a fuckin' circus out here," Ted said shaking his head.

"That it is," Leon replied. "And it's only gonna get worse if they don't find dude quick. They say he was a major figure in the Mexican Cartel. This shit makes the feds look bad."

As they made their way, a brunette reporter in her early forties approached them. Ted recognized her face from television.

"Excuse me, officers, "she called out. Her cameraman right on her heels. "May I have a word with you two?"

Ted held up a hand to shield his face from the camera. Leon, on the other hand, flashed a wide smile. "What'chu need pretty lady?"

"I'm Sandy Woods, with Fox News," she responded. "Have there been any new developments in the search for Jorge Suniga, Mexico's notorious drug boss?"

Leon stopped and faced her and the camera. With the aura of a prized winning actor accepting an award he said, "First let me say, we are doing everything to control and contain this matter. My staff and local officials are cooperating to effectively locate and apprehend the fugitive."

"May I ask your name and rank here at the prison?"

"Yes, my name is Lieutenant Ted Gibbs."

When he heard his name used, Ted laughed to himself.

"Thank you," Sandy said to Leon as she lowered her microphone.

"No problem," he replied. "If you have any more questions concerning any new developments, maybe it's possible we discuss it over dinner."

Smiling she said, "Thanks for the offer but my husband might not approve."

"Oh, well he can come too," he offered.

The cameraman lowered his equipment and said, "Nah, but thanks buddy. I'm not into men."

Still in hearing distance, Ted laughed out loud. "Man, bring your ass." Leon was laughing as well out of embarrassment.

As the two men continued into the building, Ted noticed the four plain suited men exiting. He opened the glass door, letting Leon go in first. The four men exited out of the door next to them with the first turning toward him.

"Officer Ted Gibbs?" the slim white man asked.

"Nah, that's Officer Gibbs right there," he said pointing towards Leon who tried to portray him.

But the stern faced man wasn't having it. "Officer Gibbs, sir, I'm gonna need you to put your hands behind your back."

"My what?" All of a sudden he realized that the other three men had surrounded him.

"We're from the Federal Bureau of Investigation. You're under arrest," the man said.

"Arrest?" As he spoke the other three men grabbed him. "Hey!" he yelled out angrily.

Ted saw Leon and other officers looking at the commotion. Captain McDaniels and Warden Maddox were there also. "What's this all about?"

The slim white agent said, "We have a taped confession of you admitting to orchestrating the murder of Richard Frost. Your motive revenge and jealousy."

"I didn't kill anyone," he said. Then he remembered Nurse Frost and thought about their conversations. He remembered how she was acting funny the last time they spoke. "You bitch! You set me up!"

Right before the eyes of his co-worker, Ted was arrested and hauled away. He realized how he was used as a pawn by the nurse all along. The agent explained while he was in the backseat how the confession was sent by a lawyer representing the Frost family. Not confirming anything, he sat quietly trying to figure how in the hell he got into the position he was in.

On her way to the Unit Alexis made a detour...

When she buzzed the door to the Special Housing Unit, she waited for the officer working the Central Booth to respond.

"Ms. Green....what brings you down here?" a male voice boomed over the intercom.

"Who's that?"

The secured door popped its metallic lock, allowing her to enter.

"It's Willis," came his response.

Alexis had no idea who he was but put on her best acting voice. "Oh...hey!" she replied opening the door and entering the sally port area.

Another door stood between her and the actual housing unit. Once it was unlocked, Alexis went in and saw the young black officer working the booth.

She waved. "How are you?"

He smiled. Obviously attracted to her he said, "I'm chillin' out pretty lady. What brings you by?"

"I had to pack an inmate's property a few days ago and I got some of his things mixed with his cellies," she lied. "I just wanted to ask him about a few items so I don't have to worry about him filing any grievances against me."

Willis nodded. "Yeah, you don't want a lot of complaints in your file. These inmates will file on you in a heartbeat. What's his name?"

"Peter Mosley."

The C.O. looked over a long roster and found the name. "Yeah, he's on C-Lower Range, cell eighteen."

"Thanks," Alexis smiled and said.

Making her way around the booth, she saw a few orderlies working the ranges. These inmates were the ones who'd been in the SHU the longest. A few officers were walking ranges as well seeing to inmate needs.

Willis popped the gate on C-Range and as soon as Alexis closed it she heard cat-calls from the men.

"Damn baby! Hey Roscoe!!"

A response came. "Yeah I see her."

"She thick as a brick!"

The guy speaking was to her left, and he spoke to a guy on her right. Both were in their cells naked from the waist up. She figured they may have been naked all together. When she looked at the one on her right she saw lust in his eyes.

"Damn sexy, who's you?" he asked.

She paid him no mind as she continued on looking for cell eighteen. Seeing it, Alexis stepped to the door, looking in the window. Petey Moe was sitting on his bunk reading a book and whoever was on the top bunk was gone.

"Mosely!" she called out. Petey Moe looked up and when he saw her he smiled.

"Well if it ain't Ms. Green. What's up bae, you got somethin' for me?" The wave of anger that came over her was strong.

"Yeah nigga, a new indictment. I just want you to know it was me who put that in your cell, and I hope they give you some more time."

Getting up from his bunk Petey Moe laughed and with a sneer on his face he approached the door. "Bitch, you think I didn't know that? Hoe ass tramp, that shit don't mean nothin' to me."

Now it was her turn to laugh. "Okay, we'll see. But call me another bitch and I'll show you what else I got for yo' rapist ass," she threatened.

But he didn't flinch. "You ain't got shit for me. Matter of fact, I got somethin' for you."

"You ain't got shit for me!"

He laughed. "Yes I do. I got some information and advice."

"You can keep your snitchin' ass information and advice," she said rolling her eyes.

Leaning closer to the door, he looked her dead in the eye. "Well, since I'm in a good mood today I'll give it to you anyway. I got HIV bitch....ya' best get tested," he spat with aggression.

As the flurry of curse words escaped her lips somewhere deep inside her subconscious Alexis was sickened; there was something in his eyes that troubled her soul. Something that told her he was not joking one bit.

3

The desert's sun was blazing hot and Gordo was sweating like a Mexican immigrant working in a factory for fifty cents an hour. He was nowhere in the shape he needed to be for this journey. The lofty thoughts of him traveling as a child now registered as a long ago adventure. He was now old and fat; two things that worked against him every step of the way.

The hard dirt beneath his feet seemed to stretch for miles. It had been over 24 hours with no water yet, besides his legs hurting, Gordo trekked on. With his phone, he mapped his way past small hills and ravines. The scorpions and rodents scurried and crawled all around him, and he knew many snakes were present. None frightened him more than the U.S. Marshals who were surely searching for him.

Shielding his eyes from the sun, he looked in the distant, hoping to see any sign of his convoy. The new head of the Cartel was a man named Flaco Mena. A man who rose up the ranks from a local militant. He was known to be ruthless in his dealing, and once Gordo was captured, Flaco aggressively collected all owed to the Cartel, earning him the top rank. Gordo's first call was to him, needing only aid with money and the convoy. But still he saw nothing but vultures in the distance, looking for their next meal.

Hours had passed. Once he heard a faint sound of helicopter blades cutting through the air, sending him to hide behind a collection of boulders. When he looked he saw a miniature craft yards away, flying in the opposite direction. When he felt safe enough Gordo continued on, keeping his eyes open for any signs of his people.

By the time the sun set directly at the top of the clear blue sky, Gordo was laboring heavily. His feet hurt and his legs ached. Not once had he stopped for rest and now it was showing.

"Dios, dame la fuersa," he said asking for God to give him strength. Doubling over at the waist he placed his hands on his knees, taking a breather. That's when he heard a soft roar in the wind.

At first he thought it was the sun rays, and the heat waves off the desert ground, playing tricks on him. As Gordo looked in the distance, he saw puffs of dust as they grew closer and closer. Straining his eyes, he began to see the outline of several vehicles driving his way. "Gracias!" he called to the sky. The excitement gave him new energy as he straightened himself to a comfortable march.

The closer the plumes of dust came, the faster Gordo walked, smiling with each step. Soon he was able to make out more than five vehicles. There were 3 Jeeps and 2 trucks. Each filled with the outline of men. Once they came upon him they slowed then stopped.

Elated he cried, "Mi Paisa!" His fist thrown to the sky in victory.

Armed men dressed in camouflage fatigues stood on the beds of the trucks. One of the Jeeps was outfitted with onyx black paint and tinted windows. It stood out from the other two non-descriptive Jeeps, carrying 4 dusty soldiers a piece. On cue, the rear doors to the black Jeep opened.

Gordo watched as the Cartel's new leader, and his brother-in-law, Flaco Mena, exited. Dressed in an army green suit and dark shades, his breast pocket was decorated with an assortment of metals. "Brother!" Although it has been years the man hadn't aged his 51 years.

Removing his shades, Flaco approached him. Several of his men hopped down from the trucks.

"El Jeffe", he said referring to Gordo by the name the world knew him by. "So you've escaped." The two were now face to face.

Gordo smiled. "Yes…finally free, my brother. Free to live my life, and die a free man." Despite the dust in his eyes and dryness of his mouth, he held his chin up.

Flaco looked at the distance Gordo had traveled then back at him. "No other man have I met like you. Your strength, guidance and wisdom."

The two locked eyes.

Turning to his men, Flaco barked. "Agua!"

Jumping to his command, a soldier retrieved a canister from one of the trucks and gave it to Gordo.

"Drink brother."

Gordo unscrewed the cap and raised it to his lips. The feel of the cool and wet water on his tongue was heavenly. Greedily he swallowed, letting the fluid sooth his dry throat. "Ahhh," he released.

He replaced the cap.

"But with all that wisdom," Flaco continued. "I cannot, for the life of me understand why you would think escape would be plausible."

The words shook Gordo. "Plausible? What was I to do? Remain in prison?"

Nodding the new Cartel leader mulled over the idea. "Perhaps."

"But I'm your brother-in-law! Maria's own blood! Your children's Tio!"

"You are also our ally's enemy."

Confused as to his meaning, Gordo asked, "What ally? I was a property of the U.S. Government."

"Precisely," Flaco revealed. "Since your departure the United States Government and our organization has reignited the relationships we shared in the Nineteen Eighties. Our partnership has made our Cartel the strongest it has ever been."

Hearing this infuriated Gordo. Everyone knew the relationship with the U.S. fell sour after they breached their agreements. The plan to funnel cocaine into the nations inner city grossed in the hundreds of billions. Mexico's financial state was to be restored. Something that never occurred. "How could you?"

A sinister smile spread across Flaco's face. Taking a few steps back, he put his shades back on. "Your question is a sign of your ignorance, Senor Suniga," he said. "If you haven't noticed, I'm El Jeffe now. Yes, it would've been better for you to remain in prison. You wanted nothing, remaining El Jeffe on the inside. On the outside, there is a new regime."

Listening to his words, the man once known to the world as the most ruthless drug lord Mexico had ever seen pointed his finger and opened his mouth to say something.

Just as a hail of bullets exploded into his body.

Inside the administration building everyone braced as five head officials from Washington, DC made their way to Warden Maddox's office...

Captain McDaniels straightened his tie. "Sir, they're here."

Maddox smoothed his suit coat just as the officials entered his office. Four men and one woman formed the delegate. He knew the woman from a more private setting, but for now he smiled. "Glad you all finally made it," he said, shaking each of their hands.

The Director of Bureau of Prisons, Olivia Hamilton, was a beautiful woman. With jet black flowing hair, she was driven to success by her desire to rule in an all-male profession. Seeing her old friend she nodded. "Warden, it's been a while."

Yet it has, he thought of the night he saw her last. Memories of her crème colored thighs parted limberly, unfolding for him a pussy shaven smoother than butter. "Yes Ms. Hamilton, it has been."

"Call me Olivia, please."

He knew that she was being put on the spot. Although it had been years, her being the director and his prison drawing all this attention made for a day of reckoning. He knew he had some explaining to do. "To the conference room," he said, pointing the way.

The four gentlemen were from the regional office in Grand Prairie, Texas. Once they were all seated, Maddox was asked a series of questions mostly by Olivia. The escaped prisoner was now national news and there was an ongoing investigation into possible corruption amongst his staff. But despite the question, he made sure he answered each in a manner in which assured them he was being assertive.

"We don't doubt that you'll be able to turn all this around, Trevor," she said referring to him by his first name. "I just needed to get on record your course of action."

Maddox nodded as he saw her look at the other men. "Well, I appreciate the faith."

"Listen, you're more than capable to handle any facility in our nation. We know this. Actually, our visit to you today is of another nature."

"Another nature?"

"Yes," she said, getting up from her chair the other men followed.

Maddox stood as well. His captain gave him an odd look.

"Ah , excuse me, Captain. But we won't be needing you any further."

Captain McDaniels looked at the director and said, "Yes ma'am."

Maddox didn't know what to make of this but he asked no questions. He simply followed the five officials as they led him through his own prison. Down the corridors, they walked until they came to medical. He gave Olivia a look and she nodded, as if to say this was important.

"Has there been an issue with our medical?" he asked.

She shook her head. "Hardly. Just be patient. There's more to this place then you were originally briefed on."

Now he was really confused but he knew everything would be explained so he simply followed.

Since the institution was on lockdown, the medical facility was quiet. Maddox was taken through several doors and he realized how little he actually knew about the department. On the other hand, Olivia seemed to know the place like the back of her hand. She brought the small group to a pair of elevator doors that read: OFFICIAL USE ONLY!!

"I've never seen this elevator," he said.

Olivia took the badge she wore around her neck and swiped it across a scanner. Then she pressed a series of numbers on the control pad before the red light on the console turned green. The elevator door opened. "All aboard fellas."

Maddox and the rest entered the elevator and Olivia pressed B for basement level. This he didn't understand, not knowing about any level below groundside. Just when he was about to inquire, she gave him another one of her looks.

*Ding.....*The carriage stopped and the elevator doors opened.

At first Maddox was shocked. The sub-level hallway was all white with floors that shined bright like a hospital. They stepped out and the sound of high heels click clacked before the sight of a black woman dressed in an all-white lab coat appeared.

Olivia approached her. "Doctor Wilson."

"Director Hamilton," she replied.

The two shook hands. Never in his life had he seen this woman and Maddox was beginning to wonder what in the hell was going on.

"Warden Maddox, this is Doctor Mya Wilson," Olivia explained. "She's heading our classified experiments here at our ADX Facility."

"That's what this is?" he asked looking around. He heard the prison was designated as an ADX. But never had he imagined it to be constructed beneath him.

"Yes," Olivia continued.

Maddox found himself growing angry. "Well why in the hell wasn't I briefed of this a year ago when I was promoted!"

"Because we weren't ready," Doctor Wilson said politely. She approached him and shook his hand.

"Who is we?" Somehow he felt there was a lot more to this than meets the eye.

"CDC," the doctor replied. "Our involvement in the government's interests to ….how do we say….improve and test our experiments is a matter of grave importance. We couldn't rush this project."

Project? Center of Disease Control? Maddox was lost.

Olivia tried to help him understand. "Trevor, this is known secretly as Area 52. It's funded by the government's sponsorship, testing subjects and following their responses for future developments in our military."

"But testing them how?"

The doctor chose to elaborate. "Through intravenous injections, the effects our drugs show. That way we can assign dosages that will not be in access to what is needed."

"Needed for what?" All this talk was confusing him.

Director Wilson looked at them all. "How about you all follow me."

Maddox's mind was thrown for a loop. First, he was waking up thinking he may be getting fired. Now he was being told there was a secret government experiment laboratory located beneath his prison that had been running for some time. But it was when they came to the end of the hallway and entered into another section that he paused.

"What the ….."

Olivia turned to face him. "Now Maddox, relax."

Before him, Maddox saw a large room with cells on both sides. But instead of bars these solitary rooms had thick plexiglas front windows and heavily padded rooms. In each were men strapped to the walls, naked and exposed under the bright light that shone in the cell. Each man seemed to be under the influence of something.

"Who are these men?" he asked approaching the glass window of a cell. The man inside drooled spit as his head tilted drunkenly to the side.

"They're your inmates," Doctor Wilson said as she stood next to him. "Every one of them."

THE WALL

On the other side of the glass...

His head felt as heavy as a wrecking ball. Even though he tried to lift it, he couldn't. Dino opened his eyes as much as he could but his lids were just as heavy. Barely he squinted enough to see figures standing and watching him. The people unrecognizable in his drugged state.

Where am I? he asked himself. The straps at his wrist were tight.

But there was no answer. Only the intoxicating feeling of sleep.

Established in 2012 Legit Styles Concierge is the "right connection" to meet your needs; whether business, personal, social and beyond. Everyone has a loved one that is distant and we are here to unlock your mind with our fingertips. We provide freedom from the inside by taking pride in connecting you to the outside world with our services.

-- Local numbers
-- Social Media accounts (Hi5, Tagged, FB, IG etc.)
-- Book/Magazine orders
-- Gift Services

Would you like to be an author?
We are currently accepting submissions.
Please email or mail your complete manuscript or for more info contact us:

Legit Styles Concierge
16501 Shady Grove Rd Suite #7562
Gaithersburg, MD 20898

For federal inmates email us: info@legit-Styles.com
Visit us at: www.Legit-Styles.com

Book Order Form
Legit Styles Publishing
16501 Shady Grove Rd Suite #7562
Gaithersburg, MD 20898

Name: _____   Inmate ID: _____

Address: _____

City/State: _____

QUANTITY	TITLES/AUTHORS	PRICE	TOTAL
	KINGPIN, Byron Grey	15.00	
	The Wall Season 1, Don Twan	15.00	
	Confessions of A Cheating Heart Donnie Ru and Don Twan	15.00	
	No TrustPassing, Hood & Face 1	15.00	
	Pay The Cost, Michael "Blue" Branch	15.00	
	A.B.C.G. (Anybody Can Get it) DeSean Gardner	15.00	
	Small Town Cemetery DeSean Gardner	15.00	
	Dinner Thieves, Zo Ali	15.00	
	COMING SOON!!		
	KingPin 2, Byron Grey		
	The Wall 2, Don Twan		
	No TrustPassing 2, Hood and Face 1		
	The Initial Investigation, Byron Grey		
	Murderland, Byron Grey		

Sub Total $_____   Shipping $_____   Total Enclosed $_____

Shipping & Handling (Via US media Mail) $ 3.95 1-2 book(s), $ 7.95 3-4 books, 4 books or more free shipping.

FORMS OF ACCEPTED PAYMENTS:
Certified or government issued checks and money orders, all mail in orders take 5-7 business days to be delivered. Books can be purchased by credit card at 1-800-986-0000 or on our website at www.legitstylespublishing.com. Incarcerated readers receive 25% discount. Please pay $11.25 and apply the same shipping terms stated above.

www.ingramcontent.com/pod-product-compliance
Lightning Source LLC
Chambersburg PA
CBHW031152270326
41931CB00006B/241